interview ba
flash back
hypocrisy

Julian Mitchell

"BOYS RUN THE SCHOOL"
HOW ENGLISH BROUGHT UP
BRATH

ANOTHER
COUNTRY

FORGET ALL
OLD BEAT YOUNG
ENGLISH SOCIETY
INABILITY TO CHANGE
ENGLISH DON'T LIKE CHANGE

'The experiences undergone by boys at the great public schools, their glories and disappointments, are so intense as to dominate their lives and to arrest their development. From these it results that the greater part of the ruling class remains adolescent, school-minded, self-conscious, cowardly, sentimental and in the last analysis homosexual.'

Cyril Connolly
Enemies of Promise

CANT ACROSS YUK ASS
TRY TO BEAT MY MEMORY
TWO BOYS HAVING A STORY
WORST THING ~~EXSPELL~~ EXPELL
JUSTIFY COMMUNIST
PUBLIC SCHOOL

AMBER LANE PRESS

AUTHOR
WHO WILL FEAR EVERYDAY
"I'm not a soldier — I'm a ~~schoolboy~~"

First published in 1982, reprinted 1983, 1984, 1985,
1987, 1989
Amber Lane Press Ltd.
Church Street, Charlbury, Oxford OX7 3PR

Printed in Great Britain by
Richard Clay Ltd., Bungay, Suffolk

Copyright © Julian Mitchell 1982
ISBN 0 906399 31 9

CAST

GUY BENNETT TOMMY JUDD DONALD DEVENISH }	seventeen-year-old boys in Gascoigne's house
JIM MENZIES FOWLER SANDERSON }	house prefects
BARCLAY	head of house and member of Twenty Two
DELAHAY	member of Twenty Two
WHARTON	a fag
VAUGHAN CUNNINGHAM	a literary intellectual in his forties

TIME   Summer, in the early 1930's

PLACE   An English Public School

Another Country was first produced at the Greenwich Theatre, London, on 5th November, 1981. It was directed by Stuart Burge, with the following cast:

GUY BENNETT	Rupert Everett
TOMMY JUDD	Joshua Le Touzel
DONALD DEVENISH	Piers Flint-Shipman
JIM MENZIES	David Parfitt
FOWLER	Michael Parkhouse
SANDERSON	Christopher Villiers
BARCLAY	Matthew Solon
DELAHAY	Simon Dutton
WHARTON	Gary Carp
VAUGHAN CUNNINGHAM	David William

Designed by Bernard Culshaw
Lighting by Nick Chelton

The play transferred to the Queen's Theatre, Shaftesbury Avenue, on 2nd March, 1982, with the following changes of cast:

TOMMY JUDD	Kenneth Branagh
SANDERSON	Paul Pennington
BARCLAY	Julian Wadham
WHARTON	Warren Saire/
	Alex Lowe

ACT ONE

SCENE ONE: Library

As the curtain rises on darkness we hear the sound of a whole public school singing in chapel:

'I vow to thee, my country,
  all earthly things above,
Entire and whole and perfect,
  the service of my love:
The love that asks no question,
  the love that stands the test,
That lays upon the altar
  the dearest and the best;
The love that never falters,
  the love that pays the price,
The love that makes undaunted
  the final sacrifice.'

As the hymn ends, lights come up on the Fourth Year Library of Gascoigne's. It is a tidy but shabby room, with a table and chairs, a couple of armchairs, and shelves of books. There is a seat below the window, the divisions of which are framed in Gothic arches of purple brick. BENNETT *is at the window, watching something through binoculars. He is a slightly fleshy but good-looking boy of seventeen, wearing a grey flannel suit and house tie. He doesn't turn as two similarly dressed boys of the same age come in. They are* JUDD, *short, dark and wiry — everyone's idea of a scrum-half — and* DEVENISH, *who is tall and fair.*

JUDD: [*putting down books*] Someone's love never
falters, I see.

DEVENISH: Bennett, do pull yourself together.

JUDD: But will it pay the price?

BENNETT: [*not turning*] Anything!

JUDD: What have you done with Lenin? Oh, there he
is.

> [*He fetches a bust of Lenin from where it has
> been turned face to the wall, and puts it in
> front of his place at the table.*]

You do realise it would be sacrilege to lay him
on chapel altar? Charlie Chaplain would want a
man-to-man talk with you.

BENNETT: He can marry us, if he likes. Sanctify our
passion.

DEVENISH: Bennett!

JUDD: I'm afraid he'd only tell you how men managed
without women in the war.

BENNETT: I bet he wouldn't!

DEVENISH: Don't encourage him, Judd.

JUDD: [*taking the glasses from* BENNETT] What's this?
What's this? Three o'clock from bushy-topped
tree — can it be — ? It is! Another bushy-
topped tree!

BENNETT: Give those here.

JUDD: But he's not there.

BENNETT: Not yet. But any moment now the great oak
door of Longford's will swing open on its rusty
hinges —

DEVENISH: How do you know they're rusty?

BENNETT: — and the glorious vision will step forth. He'll
stand a moment, winsomely framed in the
tumescent archway —

JUDD: The *what*?

BENNETT: — sniffing the wind like a dappled deer —

DEVENISH: Oh, my God!

BENNETT: — and then — then — he'll shoot a tender yet
burning, soft yet passionate glance across the
three hundred yards of sacred turf, hoping

against hope that I am here to receive it. And
then I shall lay my heart at his feet.

DEVENISH: He must have enormous feet if they'll stretch
from Longford's to here.

JUDD: [*handing the glasses back*] You're so stupidly
romantic. Why fall in love with the unattain-
able?

BENNETT: It's more fun. Anyway, from what I hear,
Harcourt not only *is* attainable, he's been
attained several times already.

[*He resumes watching.*]

JUDD: Only by Longford's men, surely?

BENNETT: So far.

DEVENISH: [*testy*] Bennett, did you know you're becoming
very, very boring about Harcourt?

BENNETT: [*putting the glasses down*] Am I, Devenish? I'm
terribly sorry. I bore myself practically to
extinction. I did so hope I might be mildly
amusing to my friends.

DEVENISH: Well, you're not. So stop it.

BENNETT: Can't. Sorry! One must have some spice to life
in this dingy place. [*He resumes watching*] Anyway, I'm not nearly as boring as you were about
Worsley.

[DEVENISH *looks embarrassed.*]

JUDD: You're *both* boring. And incurably bourgeois
and decadent.

BENNETT: And you're all statistics and no heart.

DEVENISH: Oh, God, don't you encourage him!

JUDD: How many times do I have to explain —

BENNETT: None — none.

JUDD: Communism is simply the logical result of
people's *feeling*.

BENNETT: [*lowering the glasses, pretending eagerness*] Each
other?

JUDD: God, you're hopeless.

BENNETT: And you're only interested in bushels per acre
in Siberia.

DEVENISH: Hectare.

BENNETT: What?

DEVENISH: Per hectare. Don't you listen to anything?

JUDD: And not Siberia.

BENNETT: Somewhere equally ghastly!

JUDD: Nowhere in the Union of Soviet Socialist Republics is ghastly.

DEVENISH: And the moon is made of green cheese. Talk about stupidly romantic!

JUDD: Vision and reason go hand in hand with us.

BENNETT: How charming! Like Jack and Jill! Who'll be the first to tumble, I wonder?

JUDD: You'll have to go, Bennett.

BENNETT: And what a struggle you'll have, fighting back your tears as you send me off! Commissar Judd! Salt mines, will it be? Or the firing squad?

JUDD: The people's court will decide.

> [MENZIES *enters. He is the same age as the others, but a prefect, which means he can wear an ordinary tie, instead of the house one, and a tweed jacket.*]

MENZIES: What now?

BENNETT: My future under socialism.

MENZIES: Oh! That!

JUDD: All punishments will be laid down in the appropriate chapters of the Soviet penal code.

BENNETT: Don't you think it's riveting, Menzies? The way he reveals his class and upbringing? All those fathers and grandfathers in the Indian Civil, carefully applying the rule-book to the Great Unwashed!

JUDD: There's no connection.

BENNETT: Bureaucracy! It's all just bureaucracy under different names. People bossing you about and collecting taxes. Underneath that anarchistic exterior —

JUDD: I am *not* an anarchist!

BENNETT: — there lurks a spirit as rigidly administrative, as predatorily imperial as — as —

MENZIES: Curzon's? Milner's?

BENNETT: You're as foul at heart as Fowler, Judd.

JUDD: Now, look, I'm prepared to put up with most things —

MENZIES: Talking of Fowler —

DEVENISH: We don't in here, if you don't mind.

MENZIES: I think I should warn you, Bennett — he's taken great exception to the state of your uniform at the Dedication.

DEVENISH: You *were* a bloody disgrace.

BENNETT: It wasn't an inspection.

DEVENISH: You should respect the dead. You'd better buck your ideas up before Jacker Pot.

BENNETT: There's no room for ideas in the corps, Devenish.

DEVENISH: You're really going to have to smarten up on parade. Pull your socks up generally.

JUDD: At least *change* them.

BENNETT: They're not too bad. Not more than a week old at most.

DEVENISH: Pooh!

MENZIES: I thought I should warn you.

BENNETT: Thanks.

JUDD: Ah! Listen to the authority behind the gentle hint! He's going to make a splendid head of house — don't you think?

MENZIES: I was only letting him know.

JUDD: Yes, yes!

MENZIES: Would you rather I didn't warn people about Fowler?

JUDD: No, no!

MENZIES: Well, then?

JUDD: It's just I liked you so much more *before* you were a prefect.

MENZIES: [*cool*] You'll like me again, I expect, when you're one yourself.

JUDD: Ha, *ha*.

DEVENISH: You're a fool, Judd. A complete idiot.

JUDD: I can't be against the class system *and* be a prefect. Even you must be able to see that.

BENNETT: A moron. A cretin.

JUDD: *You're* just looking forward to being in Twenty Two.

BENNETT: What's wrong with that?

JUDD: Twenty-two boys, out of a school of over four hundred! Electing each other to be demi-gods!

MENZIES: It's democratic. Surely you approve of that?

JUDD: A self-perpetuating oligarchy of mutual congratulation is *not* democratic!

BENNETT: [*eager*] Mutual what?

MENZIES: At least Twenty Two aren't appointed by the housemasters, like ordinary prefects. You've got to be someone.

JUDD: And who will you be, if not the House Man's choice to be head of house?

MENZIES: Well — apart from the ex-officios.

JUDD: And who will Bennett be, apart from your friend?

BENNETT: Wit, scholar, natural leader of men —

DEVENISH: He's at the top of the school. And in the Second Fifteen.

JUDD: Don't pretend *that* has anything to do with it. The whole system's utterly corrupt.

DEVENISH: My pater says being in Twenty Two makes the whole of school worthwhile.

MENZIES: We'll get you in, Devenish. [*to* BENNETT] Won't we?

BENNETT: Ssh! [*He crosses his fingers.*] *I'm* not in yet!

DEVENISH: Oh, you'll have no trouble. Heads of houses always get their first choice in. It's the seconds who have the trouble.

JUDD: How you can allow yourselves to collaborate with a —

MENZIES: Oh, do shut up! We *have* heard it before.

JUDD: Do you want something here, Menzies? If not, I'm afraid I must remind you that prefects are not supposed to loiter in Fourth Year Library.

MENZIES: Where else can I see my friends?

BENNETT: That's completely unnecessary, Judd.

[JUDD *points to 'Rules' on the wall.*]

MENZIES: [*still cool*] Have any of you seen Martineau? Farcical wants him.

JUDD: You're hardly likely to find him in here till next term.

MENZIES: No one's seen him since the Dedica.

DEVENISH: Probably with his parents.

MENZIES: Well — never mind. [*to* BENNETT] Have you looked at the Cicero yet? It's filthy.

BENNETT: Oh, good!

MENZIES: Not filthy dirty, filthy difficult.

BENNETT: Do you want the benefit of my insight during prep?

MENZIES: Come to my study. Thanks.

JUDD: Oh, and thank *you*, for the good-humoured restraint with which you exercise your power! I'm sure I speak for the whole house when I say how much we hope you'll be able to keep it up next term.

MENZIES: I can but try.

[*Smiling, he goes.*]

DEVENISH: There's no need to be so offensive, Judd. [JUDD *shrugs.*] You've got no manners whatever. [*to* BENNETT] You know what he was doing in the two minutes silence?

BENNETT: [*pretending horror*] Judd, no!

DEVENISH: Laughing.

JUDD: I was not.

DEVENISH: I could see you out of the corner of my eye. Skulking with the juniors and *giggling*.

JUDD: I didn't utter a sound.

DEVENISH: Then you were giggling *silently*. I couldn't concentrate on the dead at all.

BENNETT: [*reproachful*] Judd!

JUDD: Even a crusty old Tory like you, Devenish, must be able to see that it's absolutely ludicrous for four hundred boys to line up and blub for a lot of people they never knew, and who only died in a businessmen's war because they were too damned stupid to shoot their superior officers and start a revolution like the Russians.

BENNETT: But they *were* the superior officers, weren't they?

JUDD: We all know who *you* thought about.

BENNETT: Well, naturally.
          [*He resumes watching through the glasses.*]

JUDD: *Un*naturally, you mean.

BENNETT: All phenomena in nature are natural. Don't they teach you anything on the History Ladder?

DEVENISH: You're *both* offensive! It's a beautiful memorial. And all those names — three hundred and forty-two. Think of it. They died for *us*.

JUDD: They died for their class.

DEVENISH: You *are* their class! And it's damned silly to pretend you're not! Always trying to be different!

BENNETT: [*to* DEVENISH] Did they die for your wicked Uncle Vaughan, too?

DEVENISH: Yes!

BENNETT: It must be odd, being a conchie, knowing people are dying for you, when you refuse to die for them. It was clever of the Head Man to get him down the week after the Dedica.

JUDD: Oh, well — [*imitating*] "On the one hand — on the other hand" —

DEVENISH: It certainly wasn't *my* idea.

BENNETT: Are you ashamed of him?

DEVENISH: Yes.

BENNETT: But he's so famous. I don't think I could be ashamed of anyone as famous as that.

DEVENISH: He's all right. He's just so bloody obstinate. Like Judd.

JUDD: I'm not *pink*, thanks very much.

DEVENISH: You shouldn't have laughed. I wanted to think about all those people, and seeing you stopped me.

JUDD: I only wish I'd had the guts to laugh out loud.

BENNETT: Be kind. Our hero only wanted to shed a manly tear.

DEVENISH: There's nothing whatever to be ashamed of in weeping for the dead.
[*Embarrassed pause.*]

BENNETT: If it's any comfort, the person I actually thought about was my father.

DEVENISH: [*also embarrassed*] But he only died when you were a junior.

BENNETT: Yes, but gallantly.

DEVENISH: I'm awfully sorry —

BENNETT: It was the Easter hols. I was reading in bed one night when I heard the most peculiar noise — a sort of muffled squeaking. I thought it was the cat at first. But then it went on and on — sort of feeble and desperate at the same time. Like something trapped. So I got up and looked out into the passage. It seemed to be coming from my parents' room, and there was a light under the door, so I assumed — well, I mean, what would you have thought?

DEVENISH: Gosh!

BENNETT: I was just going back to bed to mind my own business, and feeling pretty queasy because — well, I mean, one's own parents!

DEVENISH: Awful!

BENNETT: When I quite distinctly heard my mater say, 'Help!' [*He imitates her.*] 'Help!'
[DEVENISH *is enthralled.* JUDD *is more and more sceptical.*]
It was terribly eerie. Complete silence, then suddenly there it was again. 'Help!' So — I didn't know what to do. I went down the passage to their door. I listened a moment, then I knocked and said, 'Are you all right?' And she said — [*Imitation of the muffled voice again.*] — 'Guy! Quick — help!' She sounded absolutely at her last gasp. So I turned the door handle to go in — only of course the door was locked.

DEVENISH: Of course!

JUDD: Don't overdo it, Bennett. It's really good so far.

BENNETT: It's true. Every word. I only wish it wasn't.

DEVENISH: Did you break the door down?

BENNETT: No. All the bedroom keys are the same in our house. I see why now. But it took me ages to push their key out backwards and get mine in. And then, when I finally got the door open —

DEVENISH: What?

BENNETT: — my pater had had a heart attack right in the middle of —

DEVENISH: No!

[JUDD *claps ironically.*]

BENNETT: [*turning on him*] Have you ever tried lifting your father's corpse off your living mother?

JUDD: Not recently.

BENNETT: It's incredibly difficult. He was like a huge sack of — of wet mud. The weight never went where I was expecting. And since he was — you know — still plugged in —

DEVENISH: No!

JUDD: *No.*

BENNETT: Unfortunately, yes.

DEVENISH: Does it — I mean — does it stay —

BENNETT: Rigor mortis.

JUDD: Bennett!

BENNETT: My mother kept her eyes shut the whole time. I suppose she thought if she couldn't see me, I couldn't see her. But of course I could.

DEVENISH: Couldn't she have — well — wriggled out from under?

BENNETT: Well, he was a very fleshy man. And they were in rather a complicated position. I think that's what did it. The mechanics were too much for him. There was a ghastly moment I thought I might have to break one of his arms.

DEVENISH: [*unable to imagine it*] How absolutely —

BENNETT: What made it all the more macabre was, I'd always hated him. He was a complete loather. Whereas my mother — I couldn't help thinking — it's all right for him — what better way to go?

But for *her* — and *me*, seeing her, like it says in the Bible, uncovered — I honestly wondered if we'd ever be able to look each other in the eye again. If you ask me, it's why she's marrying this awful Colonel person.

DEVENISH: I don't follow.

BENNETT: Protection. Distance. She feels naked again every time she sees me.

DEVENISH: How *awful.*

BENNETT: Well, it is, rather.
[*Pause.*]

JUDD: *Now* can I applaud?

BENNETT: At least I've seen a naked woman, which is more than you've done. [JUDD *laughs scornfully.*] No-one believes in you and your usherette.

JUDD: You can believe what you like. Quite incidentally, I don't see *what* your father's conking out has to do with the two minutes' silence.

BENNETT: He was in the Navy in the war. Torpedo officer on a destroyer. I always imagine him thinking about torpedoes as he died.

DEVENISH: [*Suddenly uncertain*] Bennett, you're not — you haven't —

JUDD: Devenish!

BENNETT: I'd rather you didn't spread it around, if you don't mind. I don't want people looking at my mater on Speech Day and thinking about *that.*

JUDD: No-one can ever look anywhere else, the hats she wears.

BENNETT: Aren't they splendid? I choose them for her.

DEVENISH: You *what?*

BENNETT: I love hat-shops.

DEVENISH: Good God! I wouldn't be seen dead in one.

BENNETT: Well, you have no eye, Devenish. Except for cricket balls.
[*He raises the glasses. As he does so the door is thrown open and* FOWLER *stands there, as though hoping to catch them in some criminal act. He is tall and sallow, a house prefect. At*

> *once,* DEVENISH *picks up a newspaper — it is the 'Daily Worker' — and reads it ostentatiously.* BENNETT *continues to look out of the window.* JUDD *pretends to be writing. They are absolutely united.*]

FOWLER: Have any of you seen Martineau?

BENNETT: } No.
JUDD: } No.

FOWLER: Sure?

BENNETT: } Yes.
JUDD: } Yes.

FOWLER: The House Man wants him. [*No response.*] What are you looking at, Bennett?

BENNETT: The beauties of nature.

FOWLER: Have you permission to use house binos?

BENNETT: Yes.

FOWLER: Who from?

JUDD: From whom, Fowler. From whom.

FOWLER: Who from, Bennett?

JUDD: No wonder he never made it beyond the Middle Fifth!

BENNETT: Farcical.

FOWLER: Who?

BENNETT: Farcical.

FOWLER: If you mean Mr Farquharson, kindly use his proper name.

JUDD: You didn't.

FOWLER: What?

JUDD: Use his proper name. You called him the House Man.

FOWLER: He is the House Man.

JUDD: I know *that.*

FOWLER: Are you trying to be clever or something?

JUDD: I don't have to try. I *am* clever.

FOWLER: Then what the hell are you talking about?

JUDD: Your habit of telling people to do one thing, then doing another yourself.

FOWLER: Insolence to prefects is a beatable offence, Judd. Even if you are in the Sixth Form.

JUDD: Ah. As Hon. Sec. of Gascoigne's Fourth Year Library Committee, Fowler, it's my pleasure to draw your attention to Rule 16B. You'll find it by your right elbow.

[*He points to the list.*]

BENNETT: [*not lowering the glasses*] That's the one you use to wield the cane.

JUDD: As you can see, Rule 16B states that all threats of corporal punishment are forbidden within the precincts of the library.

FOWLER: When was that passed?

JUDD: Immediately after you so grossly abused Devenish the last time you burst in here uninvited.

FOWLER: You can't make up rules just like that.

JUDD: Indeed not. Library is a democracy. Sixty-six and two-thirds of eligible votes are required for any rule change. This one, I'm pleased to tell you, was passed *nem. con.*

BENNETT: [*still not looking round*] Which for those in the army class means unanimously.

FOWLER: You're getting above yourself again, Bennett.

BENNETT: My favourite position.

FOWLER: Your uniform this morning was a disgrace.

BENNETT: You thought it was a bloody disgrace, didn't you, Devenish?

[DEVENISH *refuses to acknowledge him.*]

FOWLER: I've half a mind to ask Barclay for permission to beat you.

JUDD: Well — you've half a mind. We can all agree on that.

FOWLER: Right! That's it! [JUDD *points to the Rules.*] You needn't think you'll get away with this, either of you!

[*He goes abruptly, leaving the door open.*]

DEVENISH: [*yelling*] Shut the bloody door! [*He gets up and shuts it himself.*] That man is absolutely beyond belief.

BENNETT: [*lowering the glasses*] If only he were!

JUDD: He's precisely what this school was designed to produce. Not empire builders — dear me, no. Building empires needs imagination. Empire rulers.

DEVENISH: Oh, dry up.

JUDD: People like my own appalling forebears, since Bennett was so rude as to mention them. Licensed bullies. Fowler will go from the King's African Rifles straight into the Colonial Service — you wait and see. He'll end up with an OBE.

BENNETT: Will he retire to Bournemouth? Or Eastbourne?

JUDD: I think — Bexhill-on-Sea for Fowler. Where he'll die almost at once.

BENNETT: Syphilis?

JUDD: Nostalgia for his natives.

BENNETT: Oh, I did so hope he'd get syphilis! Won't he ever have sex at all?

JUDD: There'll be a leathery wife for that.

BENNETT: Will he tan her?

JUDD: He'll try it on the honeymoon, but she won't stand for it.

BENNETT: He'll take it out on the natives, then.

JUDD: Yes.

BENNETT: What about when he retires?

JUDD: Oh, there'll be a motherly little woman in South Cliff.

BENNETT: God, how drab. [*He resumes watching.*] Poor old colonies.

DEVENISH: There's nothing wrong with the Colonial Service. It's a perfectly decent career.

JUDD: There's nothing decent about colonialism.

DEVENISH: I don't see why you have to be so against everything.

JUDD: I'm not. I'm *for* revolution.

DEVENISH: That's just silly.

BENNETT: I say. Come and look at this.

JUDD: Has an eagle descended on your Ganymede?

BENNETT: [*handing* JUDD *the glasses*] Look at the door to

chapel bell-tower. They're carrying someone out.

[JUDD *looks. Pause.*]

JUDD: Good Lord.

DEVENISH: What is it?

[JUDD *hands him the glasses. Pause.*]

One of the bell-ringers must have had an accident.

[*He hands the glasses to* BENNETT.]

It can happen. The bell turns over or something, and you get swept right off your feet. One of our tenants cracked his skull a few years ago, ringing in the New Year.

JUDD: I haven't heard any bells. Not since the Dedica.

[*Pause.*]

BENNETT: You know what I think. It's Martineau.

[*He hands the glasses to* JUDD.]

DEVENISH: But Martineau's not a bell-ringer.

JUDD: [*looking*] God, I think you're right.

DEVENISH: Let me see.

[*He takes the glasses and looks. Pause. He lowers the glasses.*]

How very peculiar.

[*Pause.*]

BENNETT: Oh, God. Poor Martineau.

[*A bell is rung violently from within the house.*]

[*Blackout.*]

SCENE TWO: Barclay's study

The head of the house has only a smallish study, with room for five people to cram themselves in. There is a desk with a chair, an armchair, a bookshelf and a window-seat as in the Library.

BARCLAY, *mild and spectacled and ill-at-ease, is standing. He wears a tail coat with a buttonhole, and a fancy waistcoat, to indicate his membership of Twenty Two.* DELAHAY, *similarly dressed, is lounging in the armchair; he is big and burly, a sportsman.* FOWLER, MENZIES *and* SANDERSON *are on the window-seat.* SANDERSON *is short, with a slightly resentful air, as though determined not to be put up-on.*

Pause.

DELAHAY: From a bell-rope?
BARCLAY: Yes.
DELAHAY: He must have been mad.
BARCLAY: Well — there'll have to be an inquest.
SANDERSON: The balance of his mind —
BARCLAY: Quite.
        [Pause.]
MENZIES: Did he leave a note, Barclay?
BARCLAY: Farquharson says only the coroner need see it.
SANDERSON: Well, really!
BARCLAY: But — it seems Mr Nicolson caught him in Phot. Soc. Dark Room yesterday evening with a man in Longford's.
MENZIES: Oh, Lord.
        [Pause.]
FOWLER: What man in Longford's?
BARCLAY: Robbins.
FOWLER: I know Robbins.
        [Pause.]
DELAHAY: Silly bloody fools! What did they want to go and get caught for?
SANDERSON: I dare say they didn't actually *want* to get caught, Delahay.
DELAHAY: What was Nickers doing in Dark Room, anyway?
BARCLAY: I don't know. But he reported them both to their House Men last night, and they were

supposed to go to the Head Man immediately after the Dedica. Robbins turned up, but Martineau —
[*Pause.*]

MENZIES: Couldn't the House Men have handled it?

SANDERSON: Men in different houses? On school grounds?

BARCLAY: I'm afraid Sanderson's right. They had to be sunkered.
[*Pause.*]

MENZIES: Poor Martineau.
[*Pause.*]

DELAHAY: If you ask me, these things should be left to Twenty Two.

FOWLER: Even the mighty Twenty Two can't sunker people, Delahay.

DELAHAY: Who needs people sunkered?

FOWLER: You wouldn't let them stay?

DELAHAY: Of course. After making them run the gamut with gym shoes, for being so bloody stupid.

FOWLER: Stupid!

DELAHAY: Letting themselves get caught.

FOWLER: Delahay, really!

DELAHAY: Yes, really, Fowler.
[*Pause.*]

MENZIES: Do we — do we know what it was they were actually doing?

SANDERSON: Need you ask?

FOWLER: What possible difference could it make!

MENZIES: Well, if it was just — you know —

FOWLER: Immorality is immorality, Menzies.
[*Pause.*]

DELAHAY: If you ask me, it all comes of having masters who aren't old boys.

SANDERSON: I beg your pardon?

DELAHAY: An old boy would have more sense than to go prowling round Phot. Soc. Dark Room in the evenings.

FOWLER: [*outraged*] That's — that's absolutely —

DELAHAY: If you'd caught them , you'd have had to report

them to me or Barclay — someone in Twenty
Two. That's school practice. Men deal with
men. Once masters get involved, it's fatal. Old
boys *know* that.

[SANDERSON *suddenly giggles.*]

BARCLAY: Sanderson —

SANDERSON: Sorry. I just thought of all the ruined negatives.

BARCLAY: What?

SANDERSON: Nickers must have turned the light on,
mustn't he? No Phot. Soc. exhibition *this*
Speech Day!

FOWLER: You're in Phot. Soc., aren't you?

SANDERSON: So what?

FOWLER: Nothing.

SANDERSON: If you're accusing me —

BARCLAY: Sanderson —

SANDERSON: I'm not having him accusing me —

BARCLAY: Shut up, both of you. Someone has *died*.
[*Silence.*] His parents are coming down
tomorrow.

DELAHAY: Oh, Lord!

BARCLAY: Some of us will have to meet them. I'll go myself, of course. I don't know if any of you — ?
[*Silence.*] In that case, Delahay, you'll have to
come.

DELAHAY: What on earth can I say?

BARCLAY: I don't know. How good he was at rugger.

DELAHAY: But he wasn't.

BARCLAY: He was in Cooper Pot Fifteen.

DELAHAY: Well, all right, but — honestly!

BARCLAY: Thank you. I — I didn't know him very well
myself. Did any of you? [*Silence.*] Who were his
friends?

MENZIES: I don't think he had any special friends. He and
Bennett saw each other in the holidays sometimes.

FOWLER: Oh?

MENZIES: They lived quite close, that's all. They weren't

real friends. He went up to school in a three-
some with Howell and Rawsthorne.

BARCLAY: Perhaps they'd like to come.

MENZIES: I rather doubt it.

FOWLER: It's not a question of them liking, Barclay. If
you tell them to go, they'll go.

BARCLAY: I should prefer not to use coercion on an occa-
sion like this.

SANDERSON: Yes, for God's sake, Fowler!

BARCLAY: We — we have to consider the effect on the
house as a whole. [*Pause.*] Personally, I feel
absolutely — [*Pause.*] I've tried to make everyone feel he can come to me at any time, whatever the problem. And he must have been
desperate. But — [*Pause.*] He was even in my
dorm.

[*Long embarrassed silence.*]

SANDERSON: It wouldn't have made any difference. He'd
still have been sunkered.

BARCLAY: But if he'd talked to me — you — anyone —
[*Silence.*]

FOWLER: I think that's rot.

BARCLAY: Oh.

FOWLER: The problem is, the tone of the house has
simply gone to pieces.

DELAHAY: Fowler!

FOWLER: And you're one of the people mainly responsible! You've always acted as though school and
house rules don't apply to you!

DELAHAY: Well?

FOWLER: What kind of example is that? Captain of
Games, a member of Twenty Two, swanking
about and openly breaking the rules! The
juniors *imitate* you — don't you realise?

BARCLAY: Fowler —

FOWLER: And you do nothing to stop him! He's been a
bad influence on the house from the day he
arrived!

DELAHAY: I'll be a bad influence on you in a moment.

FOWLER: Things have got so slack — It was something to be in Gascoigne's once. Now — *now!*

BARCLAY: This is hardly the time or place to go into all that, if you don't mind.

SANDERSON: No!

FOWLER: Not when things have got so bad a man has been caught with a man in another house and then hanged himself!

[*Pause.*]

BARCLAY: You know perfectly well how we spent our first two years here, Fowler. How much beating and bullying there was.

FOWLER: At least it stopped us indulging in immorality!

DELAHAY: Don't be so bloody pi, for God's sake!

FOWLER: Delahay excepted, of course! He always is!

BARCLAY: Please — [*Silence.*] If I'm responsible, then I'm responsible. But I made a vow at the end of my first term, if I ever became head of house, I'd do my utmost to see that no-one ever had to creep about in fear and terror the way we did.

FOWLER: And now we see the result!

[BARCLAY *has no answer.*]

MENZIES: I don't see any connection between Barclay's liberal regime and Martineau's suicide. Really, I don't.

BARCLAY: Thank you.

FOWLER: Then things can only go from bad to worse here next year!

SANDERSON: Till there's no-one left alive, you mean?

DELAHAY: You're so stupid, Fowler. If Nickers hadn't broken school practice, Martineau would still be here. He'd have a very sore bum, but he'd still be here.

FOWLER: You are so corrupt, so cynical —

BARCLAY: You've had your say, Fowler.

FOWLER: But it's precisely attitudes like that —

BARCLAY: That's enough! [*Silence.*] The question isn't why it happened, but what we do now.

SANDERSON: Quite!

BARCLAY: I'm sure we can all agree at least that we don't want what happened in Warburton's happening here.

SANDERSON: God, no!

FOWLER: Warburton's has done jolly well since they had that clear-out.

SANDERSON: Mass sunkering! General hysteria! Queues to confess to the House Man! Are you mad?

DELAHAY: The *last* thing anyone wants.

FOWLER: It might be just the thing for the house in its present state.

MENZIES: If I may put a selfish point of view — I should like there still to *be* a house here next year.

SANDERSON: Quite!

FOWLER: I'm sure it's not nearly on that scale.

[*The others' silence indicates they do not share his optimism.*]

Anyway, wouldn't you rather start with a clean house?

MENZIES: Frankly, I doubt if such a thing as a clean house exists, in this school or any other.

FOWLER: Then you're as hopeless as the others!

MENZIES: I have to consider next term, Fowler. That's why I'd like hysteria kept to an absolute minimum, and all beans-spilling kept as far away from Farcical as possible.

SANDERSON: Hear, hear!

MENZIES: He'll want to be kept out of it, anyway. God, he hates even talking about it.

SANDERSON: [*imitating*] 'There are men here who may try to take advantage of a man because a man is a new man.'

MENZIES: If people start getting hysterical and rushing off behind the green baize door — that'll be *it*.

BARCLAY: Then what it boils down to is — how do we preserve the House Man's innocence?

FOWLER: Really, Barclay —

MENZIES: What about a voluntary knees-down?

DELAHAY: Don't be barmy.

MENZIES: Look, at times like this, people go religious and want to confess. Well, I think God's a much better person to hear their confessions than the House Man. Apart from anything else, the confessions are silent. All it needs is a few prayers, a lot of pi-jaw, some long pauses for thought, and a couple of cheerful hymns at the end.

BARCLAY: Well —

[*Pause.*]

SANDERSON: Menzies, you're a real brain!

DELAHAY: Can't we keep religion out of it? I mean — chapel bell-rope!

MENZIES: Of course we can't. We must just be grateful it isn't confirmation term.

SANDERSON: God, yes!

DELAHAY: Who'd take it? [*to* BARCLAY] You?·

BARCLAY: I don't know.

MENZIES: You and Fowler.

FOWLER: What?

MENZIES: You're awfully good at this sort of thing. You know you are.

FOWLER: But I don't know if I approve.

SANDERSON: I thought you always approved of everything pi.

FOWLER: If people want to go to the House Man, I think they should go.

MENZIES: If they want to, they will. None of us can stop them. This would only be a way of — well, relieving the tension.

FOWLER: But is that what the house needs at the moment?

SANDERSON: Yes!

BARCLAY: Well, I rather agree.

DELAHAY: Think of the house's reputation.

FOWLER: That's precisely what I *am* thinking about.

DELAHAY: If there's a general scandal, it won't just be all over the school, it'll be all over England. People

won't exactly be enthusiastic when we say we
were in Gascoigne's.

FOWLER: It won't get that far.

SANDERSON: It will, you know. Everyone knows everything.
Everyone who counts. My pater won't have
anyone from Harrow in the firm, because of
what he's heard.

[*Pause.*]

FOWLER: Perhaps if the knees-down were compulsory —

MENZIES: I'm afraid the Sixth wouldn't come.

FOWLER: Damn the Sixth! Make them!

MENZIES: Besides, there are new men and juniors who
won't know what it's all about. I wouldn't want
them coming.

DELAHAY: Quite.

BARCLAY: No, we don't want them.

FOWLER: Well —

BARCLAY: I think we'd all be very grateful, Fowler. You do
have a knack for this sort of thing.

FOWLER: Well — I'm not very happy about it. But if the
reputation of the house is really at stake —

BARCLAY: I think it is.

FOWLER: All right, then. After prep?

BARCLAY: Thank you.

MENZIES: Yes, thank you, Fowler.

DELAHAY: [*rising*] Bags I do dorms!

[*Blackout.*]

*In the darkness we hear a chapel full of boys reciting
the General Confession, led by* FOWLER.

SCENE THREE: Dormitory

*There are five beds in a row, each with a wash-stand
and press.* BARCLAY'S *bed has a pitch-pine partition
between it and* JUDD'S. *After* JUDD'S *there is a very
neatly made bed and a wash-stand with no toothbrush*

or flannel, etc. It was Martineau's bed. Then comes Spungin's, then WHARTON's.

WHARTON, *the dorm fag, is thirteen, his voice unbroken. He is in striped pyjamas and a camel dressing gown. He is hovering anxiously by Spungin's wash-stand, carrying a large white enamel jug with a blue rim.* BENNETT *comes quickly in, looking over his shoulder.*

BENNETT: Spungin? Wharton, have you seen Spungin?
WHARTON: No.
BENNETT: Oh, God!

> [BENNETT *hurries out again.* WHARTON *hesitates, then decides to pour water for himself. As he's about to do so,* JUDD *enters.*]

JUDD: After you, Wharton.

> [*At once* WHARTON *stops pouring and starts to take the water over to* JUDD's *basin.*]

I said, *after* you. [WHARTON *stops, uncertain.*] You really must learn that whatever anyone else does in this horrible place, when *I* say something, I mean it.

WHARTON: Sorry, Judd.
JUDD: What for?
WHARTON: I — I don't know. Sorry.
JUDD: Stop saying it!

> [*He takes the jug and starts prodding* WHARTON *back to his own cubicle.*]

One reason the proletariat is so exploited, Wharton, is its fatal fatalism. The way it *expects* the worst.

WHARTON: Yes, Judd.
JUDD: So don't connive at your own oppression. Don't assume that just because you're a fag you *must* be in the wrong. Resist the tradition!

> [*He pours water out for* WHARTON.]

WHARTON: Thank you, Judd.
JUDD: *From* those with the greatest means, *to* those with the greatest need. *Not* school practice. But

then school practice is simply designed to make
people like you say 'Sorry' the whole time.

WHARTON: Yes, Judd.

JUDD: Yes, because you understand what I'm saying
and agree with it? Or because I'm a fourth year
and you're a first?

WHARTON: [*thinks*] I'd like to get on and wash now, if you
don't mind.

JUDD: Hopeless!

> [*He carries the jug back to his own cubicle.*
> DELAHAY *enters. He has a squash ball which
> he bounces off the walls.*]

DELAHAY: God, it's all quiet on the Western Front tonight
all right!

JUDD: Has the whole house gone?

DELAHAY: Practically.

> [*He drops the ball under Martineau's bed.*]
> Damn!
> [*He grovels for it. When he comes up again he
> looks at the bed and wash-stand.*]

God, that was quick. Who did it?

JUDD: I don't know.

WHARTON: Excuse me, Delahay.

DELAHAY: Yes?

WHARTON: Matron came and cleared everything out.

DELAHAY: [*edging away*] Was he blubbing a lot last night?

JUDD: No sign anything was wrong at all.

DELAHAY: Poor sod. Still, it's a cad's trick, suicide. It just
leaves everyone feeling awful and knowing it's
too late to do anything about it.

JUDD: They can see it never happens again.

DELAHAY: Easier said than done.

JUDD: In a properly ordered society it wouldn't happen at all.

DELAHAY: Drivel. People'll always go mad.

JUDD: It's not madness. It's sense. A response to the
intolerable strains of capitalist society.

DELAHAY: Oh, I suppose in *Russia,* no-one *ever* kills himself!

JUDD: Statistics show far fewer suicides take place than before the revolution. For the obvious reason that there are far fewer social and economic contradictions and so far less strain.

DELAHAY: Are you trying to tell me Martineau was suffering from social and economic contradictions?

JUDD: Of course. This whole place is *based* on contradictions. It's a complex network of irreconcilable values. The only surprising thing is how few suicides there are.

DELAHAY: If you hate it so much why don't you leave?

JUDD: Because till I get my scholarship to Cambridge I'm in economic servitude to my parents, like everyone else.

DELAHAY: Run away. Get yourself a job.
[*He settles on* JUDD's *bed.*]

JUDD: Then how would I get my scholarship? It's difficult enough trying to work *here*. Farcical tries to stop me at every opportunity.

DELAHAY: God, you're ungrateful. He let you oil out of the Corps.

JUDD: The Corps is supposed to be voluntary.

DELAHAY: Supposed!

JUDD: And he *won't* let me off games.

DELAHAY: I should hope not. Games are good for bolshies. Teach you a bit of team spirit.

JUDD: But cricket's *three* afternoons a week!

DELAHAY: You could be quite good, if you'd only try.

JUDD: I'd rather *work*. And people won't let me. I don't interfere with them, why do they have to interfere with me? Barclay confiscated another torch last night.

DELAHAY: Well, you will be so bloody obvious. When you hear someone coming you should turn the damned thing off.

JUDD: I was too absorbed in my book.

DELAHAY: [*picking it up and looking at it*] *Das Kapital*! Serves you bloody well right!

JUDD: You don't actually believe in rules, do you?

DELAHAY: What?

JUDD: You think they're only there to be *seen* to be obeyed.

DELAHAY: Depends who you are. If you can ride 'em, ride 'em. If not — watch out!

JUDD: What a hypocrite you are. [*He washes his face.*] Martineau wasn't a hypocrite. That's why he did it. This ghastly school persuaded him its footling, meaningless rules actually stood for something real. [*He splashes his face angrily.*] Moral principles! Rules of *life*!

> [BENNETT *enters in dressing-gown, very furtive. He doesn't see* DELAHAY *sitting on* JUDD's *bed.*]

BENNETT: Judd! Have you seen Spungin?

JUDD: No.

BENNETT: Oh, God! Where the hell *is* he?

DELAHAY: [*rising*] At the knees-down. And what the hell are you doing out of your dorm without permission?

BENNETT: Looking for you to ask permission to visit this one.

DELAHAY: What do you want with Spungin, anyway?

BENNETT: Nothing — nothing.

JUDD: Oh, Bennett, no!

BENNETT: [*injured innocence*] What do you mean?

JUDD: Is there no depth to which you won't sink?

BENNETT: [*sinking to Martineau's bed, head in hands*] I don't *think* so.

DELAHAY: I don't think you'll find sitting there helps your conscience.

BENNETT: What? [*He gets hurriedly up and moves away.*] You are *sure* that's where he is?

DELAHAY: Positive.

BENNETT: He hasn't been behind the green baize door?

DELAHAY: No. No-one's been. Stop being so windy.

BENNETT: Thank God!

JUDD: Of course, there's nothing to stop people going to Farcical *after* the knees-down.

[BENNETT *groans.*]

DELAHAY: Don't be cruel to dumb animals, Judd. [*to* BENNETT] Is it quiet up there?

BENNETT: As the grave.

DELAHAY: [*moving off*] Better go and see, I suppose.

BENNETT: Can I stay and talk to Judd, please?

DELAHAY: If you can get a word in. [*finding* WHARTON *hovering*] What do you want?

WHARTON: Excuse me, Delahay, what should I do about Spungin's water?

DELAHAY: What?

WHARTON: If I pour it, and he doesn't come up, it'll get cold.

DELAHAY: [*leaving*] True! True!

[WHARTON *is left even more anxious.*]

JUDD: You haven't really been having Spungin, have you?

BENNETT: Ssh!

JUDD: But he's got such awful shag-spots!

BENNETT: *Ssh!* No — I haven't.

JUDD: Well, you do have *some* taste, then.

BENNETT: If you really want to know, he repulsed my advances. That's why I'm so —

[*He takes a hip-flask from his pocket and drinks quickly.*]

JUDD: I didn't know you ever had failures.

BENNETT: Want a swig?

JUDD: Thanks. Except with me, of course.

[*He drinks.*]

BENNETT: Everyone gives in in the end. It's Bennett's Law. You just have to put the idea in their heads, and give it time to grow. People get bored with frigging. And lonely. They long for company. Like my mother. [*He drinks.*] God, it really makes me sick, her marrying that oaf.

JUDD: Then don't turn up for the wedding.

BENNETT: And miss all that champagne? Anyway, she'd be dreadfully upset. We're very close, you know. The parting's bound to be very painful.

JUDD: Won't you be gaining a father, rather than losing a mother?

BENNETT: God, I hope not! One was enough!

JUDD: Was any of that true, by the way? About your real father?

BENNETT: Bits. [JUDD *laughs.*] I couldn't help myself. Devenish is such a fool, he believes anything you tell him.

JUDD: Well, I think you should follow your mother's example. Distance yourself from the relationship with a member of the opposite sex.

BENNETT: Is it really so different?

JUDD: How would I know? I've only ever had girls.

BENNETT: [*incredulous*] Oh, come on!

JUDD: I discovered I liked girls when I was eleven. The male body has never attracted me in the slightest.

BENNETT: It might if you let it. [*earnest*] You ought to try everything once, you know.

JUDD: I wouldn't mind having every girl in the world once.

BENNETT: I'm serious.

JUDD: So am I. You should try girls.

BENNETT: I have done. Tried, I mean. I thought I was really getting somewhere last hols. I had my hand on her breast, and she didn't seem to mind. Only — it wasn't her breast. It was a hankie stuffed in her bra. She was only letting me do it because she didn't realise.

[JUDD *laughs.* WHARTON *has come to hover.*] Wharton! This is a strictly adult conversation! I hope you're not listening!

WHARTON: Oh, no! No!

JUDD: What is it, Wharton?

WHARTON: It'll be Last Post soon. I don't know what to do about Spungin's water.

BENNETT: Leave him to pass it on his own. Have a drink.

[*He offers the flask.* WHARTON *is horrified.*]

JUDD: Bennett —

BENNETT: Go on. Do you good.

WHARTON: No, thank you, Bennett.

BENNETT: Suit yourself.

> [*He drinks.*]

JUDD: [*to* WHARTON] If I were you, I'd pour it out, then go to bed.

WHARTON: But it'll be cold.

BENNETT: Serve him right for being so bloody pi.

WHARTON: He makes a terrible fuss if his water's cold. He said he'd report me to Barclay.

JUDD: [*with a sigh*] Then go and fill up the jug with new hot water, bring it back, cover it with a flannel, and leave it by his basin.

WHARTON: Whose flannel?

JUDD: *His* flannel.

WHARTON: Do you think that'll be all right? Honestly?

JUDD: *Yes.*

WHARTON: Thank you, Judd.

> [*He goes, carrying the jug.*]

BENNETT: Honestly! Juniors!

JUDD: Poor bloody child — scared to death of *Spungin.*

BENNETT: I'm fairly scared of him myself at the moment.

JUDD: You shouldn't offer him drink.

BENNETT: Why not? He's too young for anything else. I'm not a *pederast,* you know.

JUDD: Discretion is going to be the better part of valour in this place for a while, wouldn't you say?

> [DELAHAY, *entering, hears this.*]

DELAHAY: Now who's the hypocrite!

JUDD: If an objective analysis of a situation shows hypocrisy to be the correct means by which a desired end is to be achieved —

DELAHAY: Bolshies! Honestly! You'd better go back to your dorm, Bennett — they'll be up soon.

BENNETT: Three more minutes?

DELAHAY: Well — I suppose so. [*seeing someone off-stage*] Here! Howell! What the hell do you think you're doing?

                       [DELAHAY *goes.* BENNETT *brings out his flask*
                       again, drinks then hands it to JUDD.]

BENNETT: Here — finish it.

JUDD: Thanks, but I want to be able to see to read.

BENNETT: [*looking at the bookmark*] I say, you're making progress.

JUDD: I'd've finished by now, if I was only allowed to *work*!

BENNETT: I thought it was supposed to be so terribly difficult.

JUDD: I haven't found anything I couldn't understand eventually. If they taught us any economics here, instead of Tudors and bloody Stuarts — Marx should be a set book for the Sixth. They shouldn't leave us to fight our way through it on our own, *and* under the blankets. [*Pause.*] Lost another torch last night.

BENNETT: How many's that?

JUDD: Twelve. *Twelve* torches. Taken away to stop me getting the education I'm *supposed* to be here for!

BENNETT: Well — you have my sympathy.

JUDD: I don't *want* sympathy. I want intelligent treatment. I happen only to need six hours' sleep a night. That means I wake up every morning at half-past *four*. It's all right in the summer — it's soon light enough to read. But in the winter — and next term, when I'll really be swotting for the scholarship —

BENNETT: It's entirely your own fault. If you weren't so bolshie you could read as much as you like. You'd be a prefect by now. You'd probably be head of house next term, instead of Menzies.

JUDD: I keep telling my parents — if only I was at home, I could get in three hours more a day. But of course they won't listen. School keeps me out of the way — that's all they care about.

BENNETT: God, if our parents knew what actually went on here!

JUDD: They do know. The fathers, anyway.
[*Pause.*]

BENNETT: This awful Colonel of my mother's says public schools go on too long.

JUDD: They shouldn't go on at all.

BENNETT: He says we should leave when we're seventeen and take a job for a year or two. [*in imitation*] 'Go round the world. Learn a bit about life before you go up to the Varsity.' [*in his own voice*] Why not the army, I said? One learns so much about life in the army, killing people. [JUDD *laughs.*] For a moment he almost liked me. [*Pause.*] Barclay wants me to go and meet Martineau's parents.

JUDD: *You?*

BENNETT: We used to meet in the holidays sometimes. At parties and things.

JUDD: Will you go?

BENNETT: Do you think I should?

JUDD: How much did you really like him?

BENNETT: Well — I didn't *mind* him, I suppose. [*Pause.*] Actually —

JUDD: Oh, Bennett! Not him, too!

BENNETT: No! No! [*Pause.*] The thing is — I don't know what I might not say.

JUDD: Then you'd better *not* go.

BENNETT: On the other hand — if they'd like it — it wouldn't really be hypocrisy, would it?

JUDD: Yes.

BENNETT: My mother liked it when people wrote to her about my father.

JUDD: My dear Bennett, whenever people say something wouldn't *really* be hypocrisy — or lying — or cheating — it means they're half-gone already.

BENNETT: Half-gone where?

JUDD: If you practise hypocrisy without admitting it you end up not remembering what's true and what isn't. What's right and what's wrong. And if you forget that — well, you've had it as a human being, haven't you?

BENNETT: Have I?

JUDD: Almost everyone in this country *has* forgotten. They literally don't know how to be honest, decent, truthful — ordinarily human and good. That's why there *has* to be a revolution.

[DELAHAY, *entering, hears this.* WHARTON *follows him, bearing the jug of water.*]

DELAHAY: Not that again! Bennett, go to bed, before your lovely mind is as corrupted as your filthy body.

BENNETT: All right.

[*He rises. He looks at Martineau's bed.*]

You really think I shouldn't go, then?

JUDD: Up to you.

BENNETT: Well, I'm glad I'm not Robbins, anyway.

DELAHAY: What?

BENNETT: [*going*] They'll toss him on the funeral pyre, won't they?

DELAHAY: For God's sake!

BENNETT: Of course, they'll have to chop the offending member off first.

DELAHAY: That's not funny.

BENNETT: Oh, don't you think so? Good night, Judd.

JUDD: Good night.

[DELAHAY *and* BENNETT *go.* WHARTON *has deposited the jug by Spungin's basin and covered it with a flannel. But he doesn't go back to his bed. He hovers by* JUDD's *cubicle.* JUDD *is deep in 'Das Kapital'. At last he looks up.*]

Yes?

[WHARTON *bursts into tears.* JUDD *gets quickly out of bed and goes to him.*]

Whatever's the matter? You're not still worrying about that damned water, are you?

WHARTON: [*wailing*] I want my mother!

JUDD: Oh, dear, oh dear —
[*He tries to comfort him.* WHARTON *weeps on his shoulder.*]
Come on. What is it?

WHARTON: It's — it's — it's Martineau.

JUDD: What about him?

WHARTON: He — he was always very nice to me.

JUDD: Was he?

WHARTON: [*in floods of tears*] And now — now —

JUDD: [*putting his arm round* WHARTON] There, there. There, there.

WHARTON: He said — he said, I wasn't to worry. My first day. He said it was awful for everyone. Always. I hadn't been to a prepper, you see. Not a boarding one. He said — he said it would soon get better.

JUDD: And did it?

WHARTON: Oh, yes. Yes.

JUDD: Well, that was very nice of him. Come on, you ought to be in bed.
[*He starts leading* WHARTON *to his bed.*]

WHARTON: He — he wasn't ever nice like that to me again. But he was then. I shan't forget it, Judd.

JUDD: You mustn't.

WHARTON: He could see how unhappy I was, you see. It was really *kind* of him.

JUDD: Very kind indeed. Come on. Pop in.
[*They have got to* WHARTON'*s bed.* WHARTON *is helped off with his dressing-gown.*]

WHARTON: *I* was wanting to die when he said that. I thought I wasn't going to be able to bear it. Not possibly. And then he —
[*He weeps again, but more quietly. Pause.*]

JUDD: [*letting him cry, patting his back*] We all want to die sometimes. It's because other people have power over us which they have no right to. Power to make us miserable. To stop us being ourselves. Into bed now. [WHARTON *gets into bed.*] What *you* have to do, when they make you feel

like that, is say to yourself — they've no right,
no right at all. I'm *me*. I *won't* be what they want
me to be. And keep on saying it till you're really
angry.

WHARTON: Yes, Judd.

JUDD: They can beat our bottoms till they're purple
and blue. But if we keep our anger up, they'll
never get *us*. They'll never get our souls. They'll
never succeed in making us really want to die.
[*Pause.*]

WHARTON: Thank you, Judd.

JUDD: Now snuggle down and I'll tuck you up.
[WHARTON *does so.* JUDD *tucks him in.*]
There!
[JUDD *gives him a quick, fatherly kiss.*]
Good night, Wharton.

WHARTON: Good night. And — thank you, Judd.
[JUDD *goes back to his own bed. He settles
down and opens 'Das Kapital'.* DELAHAY
*watches from the door, waits till he has found
his place, then shouts:*]

DELAHAY: Last Post!
[*He switches out the light.*]

*In the darkness a cornet plays the 'Last Post'.
Suddenly it is overwhelmed by the 'Wedding March'.*

SCENE FOUR: Library

It is night. JUDD, *in pyjamas, is reading by a carefully
shaded light. Pause. There is a sudden noise outside
the window.* JUDD'S *hand goes instantly to the light
switch. The scrabbling sound continues. He leaves the
light on and goes to the window.*

BENNETT: [*off, in a loud whisper*] Hell!
[JUDD *waits a moment, then pounces as*

> BENNETT *is half in and half out of the window.*]

JUDD: [*imitating* FOWLER, *in a low whisper*] All right, Bennett! I've got you this time!

> [*For a moment* BENNETT *thinks it really is* FOWLER. *Then he relaxes and hauls himself in. He is wearing tails, fancy waistcoat and buttonhole, just like a member of Twenty Two.*]

BENNETT: God, I thought you were Fowler!

JUDD: Ssh! What on earth are you doing?

BENNETT: Celebrating!

JUDD: But I thought you didn't have to be back till tomorrow morning.

BENNETT: [*brushing himself down*] That drainpipe's a bloody disgrace. Someone should have a word with Farcical.

JUDD: Ssh!

BENNETT: Tommy — may I call you Tommy, Tommy?

JUDD: If you want.

BENNETT: Tommy — I'm in love.

JUDD: That's not exactly news.

BENNETT: I don't mean 'in love', I mean *in love*.

JUDD: You're drunk.

BENNETT: It's *like* being drunk. Only instead of things going round and round, they're perfectly, beautifully still. And not blurred — sharp — clear — brighter colours than you've ever seen. It's — it's unbelievable.

JUDD: The wedding was a success, then.

BENNETT: It wasn't a wedding. More — an engagement party.

JUDD: What? But —

BENNETT: Oh, you mean the *wedding*! That was *ghastly*. Mother blubbed. And Arthur — he wants me to call him *Arthur*, can you believe it?

JUDD: Perhaps it's his name.

BENNETT: I told her — *you* can call him anything you like,

BENNETT: he's *your* husband, I shall call him Colonel, and that's that.

JUDD: Ssh!

BENNETT: Leaving me to rot in this jail of a school, while she flaunts herself up and down the Riviera with that — that —

JUDD: *Ssh!*

BENNETT: Sorry, but — I mean, really! It's so undignified, people that age going off to Cap Ferrat. They should creep down to Cromer, and think themselves lucky. Tweeds and plus-fours and out on the links all day — that's what they should be doing. I told them so. Made mother blub *again*.

JUDD: Cad!

BENNETT: But they're trying to get rid of me, Tommy! They've got a world tour all set up — Cape Town, Singapore, Hong Kong — *Australia*! I ask you!

JUDD: Really!

BENNETT: It's the Martineau business. They fear for my moral character.

JUDD: Bit late for that, isn't it?

BENNETT: You must be mad, I said. I'm not leaving *now*. School's just getting to the good bit.

JUDD: I didn't know there was a good bit.

BENNETT: Oh, well, for you there isn't. You're determined not to have one. But for sensible people — *me* — I'm going to dress like this every day next term, Tommy.

JUDD: [*dry*] You'll have to be careful not to get any more food on the waistcoat, then. It's grubby already.

BENNETT: Damn the waistcoat. I've been waiting for this ever since my first day at prepper.

JUDD: How pathetic.

BENNETT: Nothing'll be as good again till I'm Ambassador in Paris.

JUDD: Childish.

BENNETT: Life is ladders. That's all. Prepper to here. First form to sixth. Second assistant junior Under-secretary to Ambassador in Paris. Sir Guy Bennett, GCMG, GCVO, Knight of Grace of St John of Jerusalem, Chain of the Most Exalted Order of the Queen of Sheba —

JUDD: Contemptible sycophant in the service of the bourgeoisie!

BENNETT: What?

JUDD: Contemptible sycophant in the service of the bourgeoisie! It's what Lenin called the renegade Karl Kautsky.

BENNETT: Did he, indeed!

JUDD: Because he substituted eclecticism and sophis-try for dialectics.

BENNETT: Well, that *is* bad, of course.

JUDD: And wholly failed to see that personal opportunism always and inevitably leads to subservience to the ruling class.

BENNETT: Ah, but what Lenin wholly failed to see was, I shall *be* the ruling class.

JUDD: Oh, yes? Grovelling about to kings and queens, walking backwards and kissing hands! Lenin understood all right! You're utterly imbued with the spirit of servility.

BENNETT: You mean — he wouldn't have liked me?

JUDD: No.

BENNETT: What about James?

JUDD: Who's James?

BENNETT: Harcourt. His name's James.

JUDD: Frankly, I don't think he'd have cared much for the pair of you.

BENNETT: Well, I'm not mad about him either. Lenin, I mean. James — when I got back from the wedding, I took James to dinner at the 'Fox and Hounds'.

JUDD: You're mad!

BENNETT: We arranged it all yesterday. If my mother was

marrying *Arthur*, I didn't see why I shouldn't have dinner with James. He told his House Man his uncle was coming down. [*sudden thought*] I am a fool. I should have booked a room.

JUDD: [*thinking it's just another story*] Why not the bridal suite?

BENNETT: [*serious*] No. No, that would have spoiled it. And anyway, he had to be in by nine-thirty. We wouldn't have had time.

JUDD: My God! You really did go!

BENNETT: You know, till now, it's all just been a game. Manoeuvring for glances, meeting accidentally-on-purpose. It was simply relieving the bore-dom. But now —

JUDD: You'll be sunkered.

BENNETT: No, no.

JUDD: Masters drink at the 'Fox and Hounds'. [BENNETT *shrugs.*] Bennett, you *are* mad.

BENNETT: [*picking up the binoculars*] Do call me Guy. It's so stupid, surnames. Have you ever really been in love?

JUDD: No.

BENNETT: It's — [*Pause.*] I've been walking about. Thinking. What time is it now?

JUDD: Getting on for one.

BENNETT: Three hours!

JUDD: Why didn't you come back here?

BENNETT: Because I've got an exeat. I'm free! I'm not here at all, I'm in London!

JUDD: Ssh, for God's sake! You'll get us both beaten!

BENNETT: They can't beat me if I'm not here!
        [*He laughs.*]

JUDD: *Ssh!*

BENNETT: I think I'll sleep in here, if you don't mind.

JUDD: You'd better not let anyone find you dressed like that. You'll get the gamut for that waist-coat.

BENNETT: [*stretching out on the window-seat*] When I'm in Twenty Two I'll have a fag to keep it clean. Everything will be absolutely — [*He yawns.*] Oh, Tommy! *Amor vincit omnia!*

JUDD: You're hopeless. A totally hopeless case.

BENNETT: Don't worry about me. I shan't disturb you. I'm asleep already.

[*Pause.*]

JUDD: Do you honestly think this is wise? [*Pause.*] If you're really *not* drunk, I do think — [*Pause.*] Oh, well, it's nothing to do with me.

BENNETT: Bliss!

JUDD: First they take away my torches. Then, when I take my life, or at least my bum, in my hands, and creep down here — they send me *you*. This place is impossible!

[*He switches off the light.*]

BENNETT: [*drowsy*] Good night!

JUDD: Good night!

[*He goes. Pause. Then* BENNETT *begins to sing 'Who stole my heart away'. He rises. He begins to dance.*]

End of Act One

ACT TWO

SCENE ONE: Barclay's study

The stage is dark as the curtain rises.

BARCLAY: [*in the darkness*] Fag!
    [*There is a stampede of feet across the stage. Pause. Then lights up.* BARCLAY *is standing looking out of his window.* MENZIES *comes to the door.*]

MENZIES: You wanted me?

BARCLAY: Oh, Menzies — yes. Come in. Farcical's in a tizz about this uncle of Devenish's.

MENZIES: Vaughan Cunningham?

BARCLAY: We've got to give him tea after his lecture.

MENZIES: Oh.

BARCLAY: Only he'll want Devenish to be there, naturally, and it's against house practice for non-prefects to join in Prefects' Tea, and the last thing I want at the moment is to have to entertain some bloody pacifist writer — the day before Jacker Pot, too! Whose stupid idea was *that*?

MENZIES: The Head Man's, I think.

BARCLAY: Well, why can't *he* have him to bloody tea?
    [*Pause.*]

MENZIES: What do you want me to do?

BARCLAY: Have tea with him and the Fourth Year in Library.

MENZIES: What?

BARCLAY: Someone's got to. They're your year. And

Farcical's got the wind up about him wearing suede shoes or something.

MENZIES: But —

BARCLAY: I can hardly send Fowler or Sanderson, can I?

MENZIES: But Library don't have their own tea!

BARCLAY: Today they do. They have ours.

MENZIES: That's not house practice!

BARCLAY: As a matter of fact, it is. It's what happened when General Aubrey came and Aubrey wasn't a prefect. My first year.

MENZIES: Oh.

[*Pause.*]

BARCLAY: Farcical's like a cat on hot bricks. If we don't hold on to Jacker Pot tomorrow —

MENZIES: We will. The whole house is shining boots and brasses.

BARCLAY: Shut the door, Jim.

[*Change of tone.* BARCLAY *is very depressed.* MENZIES *shuts the door.*]

Take a pew. [MENZIES *sits*] I'm leaving you the most frightful mess, I'm afraid.

MENZIES: That's all right.

BARCLAY: I've just discovered something awful. Farcical's thinking of asking Fowler to stay on a term to be head of house.

MENZIES: *What*? But he can't!

BARCLAY: Well — it's all to do with next year's prefects.

MENZIES: What about them?

BARCLAY: Devenish may be leaving at the end of this term.

[*Pause.*]

MENZIES: Since when?

BARCLAY: Since — Martineau.

[*Pause.*]

MENZIES: Oh, my God. Where do I get my fourth prefect?

BARCLAY: Exactly. The excuse is, if he's going to be a farmer, or manage the estate, or whatever, he might as well go to Agricultural College straight away. But actually — his parents take a very dim view of what's been going on here. And they're hopping mad about his bloody uncle being invited down.

MENZIES: Oh, *no*!

BARCLAY: It couldn't be worse timing. He's the ripest of fruit, apparently. Anyway, the net result is — you're going to be a prefect short. Unless you can get Judd to take a more responsible attitude.

MENZIES: Fat chance! [*Pause.*] If Farcical tries to put Fowler in above me — *I'll* refuse to be a prefect!

BARCLAY: You could certainly try that. He can't possibly afford to have two senior men who aren't prefects. It's all right about Judd — he's a school joke. But you —

MENZIES: A lot of the juniors admire Judd, actually.

BARCLAY: Well, that's another problem I've left you. I am sorry, Jim. As far as I can see I've been a total failure.

MENZIES: Oh — nonsense.

BARCLAY: I've been thinking perhaps I shouldn't wait until the end of term, but leave *now*. Before I do any more damage.

MENZIES: [*thinking furiously, not paying attention*] Don't be ridiculous.

BARCLAY: I can't get Martineau out of my head. I've never even been up Chapel Tower. But — I can't sleep: Every time I close my eyes, I see him hanging there. [*Pause.*] I'm beginning to think I shall never get him out of my mind.

MENZIES: It wasn't your fault. Really it wasn't.

BARCLAY: I don't know. [*Pause.*] I was so proud of Gascoigne's. We seemed to be such a decent, civilised bunch, on the whole.

MENZIES: We are.

BARCLAY: I feel pretty suicidal myself at the moment. I get up at night and look at his empty bed. [MENZIES *is shocked.*] You don't think Fowler could be right?

MENZIES: Never!

BARCLAY: Perhaps it would do the house good to have a purge. [*Pause.*] I'm certainly not — immaculate. Are you?

MENZIES: I don't think it's something people should talk about.

BARCLAY: Well — perhaps I *am* more contaminated than others.

MENZIES: I doubt it very much.

BARCLAY: [*with a sigh*] I can't wait for term to be over. And I was looking forward to it so much!
[*Pause.*]

MENZIES: Can Devenish be persuaded, do you think?

BARCLAY: It's not really up to him. It's his parents.
[*Pause.*]

MENZIES: Damn Judd! He's so bloody straight. He's not really open to temptation, is he?

BARCLAY: What were you thinking of?

MENZIES: Twenty Two.
[*Pause.*]

BARCLAY: I'd be jolly careful about who you put up for Twenty Two. The Free Spirits can always outvote the Ex-Officios. And given Judd's reputation —

MENZIES: He'd make a very good prefect, actually — damn him!

BARCLAY: I'm terribly sorry, Jim. It's all I can say. I'm just dreadfully sorry about everything.

[*Blackout.*]

In the darkness a jangle of pianos can be heard — boys practising scales, 'The Merry Peasant', 'The Moonlight Sonata', and jazz vamping (to say nothing of 'Chopsticks').

SCENE TWO: Library

JUDD *is working at the table. It is late afternoon.*
BENNETT *comes bursting in, carrying books. He looks*
scruffy even by his own standards. He stops short.

BENNETT: You *did* cut it!

JUDD: Of course.

BENNETT: But the Head Man told us to do an appraisers!
[*He dumps the books on the table.*]

JUDD: I don't have to hear Vaughan Cunningham to
be able to appraise him right down to his little
liberal slippers.

BENNETT: He was damned good!

JUDD: The Post War Crisis in Art and Life! Collapse of
faith in public values! Nothing left but to trust
in personal relations! Avoid politics at all costs!

BENNETT: There's much more to it than that!

JUDD: Oh, yes! Damn the old, damn the poor, damn
the unemployed! The children with rickets, the
miners coughing their lungs up! Oh, and
please don't mention the boring old Means
Test to *me*, I'm a *writer*!

BENNETT: That's just stupid. What he said was —

JUDD: [*in imitation*] 'It is the act of the civilised man in a
time of public turmoil to turn to the private life.
What I recommend is letter-writing. Pull up a
cosy chaise-longue and settle down with pen
and paper to the composition of a *minor* master-
piece, full of spice and semi-colons — and
sudden little insights between dashes — to one
of the dearest of one's dear, dear friends —
someone one can trust to show it round to all *his*
dear, dear friends, then file it away for posterity.
Though I do recommend keeping a copy one-
self, just in case. It would be too sad if posterity
were to be denied the shallow, smelly,

sentimental, morally putrid contents of the
Victorian wickerwork waste-paper basket one
is pleased, nay delighted, to call one's mind.'

BENNETT: Oh — shut up!

> [BENNETT *bangs out.* JUDD *gets on with his
> work. After a moment the door opens and*
> MENZIES *looks in.*]

MENZIES: Oh, Lord, hasn't he started even?

JUDD: Who?

MENZIES: Wharton.

JUDD: Started what?

MENZIES: Laying. Devenish is bringing his uncle to tea
with you.

JUDD: *What*?

MENZIES: Farcical's instructions.

JUDD: Bringing him *here*?

MENZIES: Even here.

JUDD: But I'm working!

MENZIES: Then you must stop.

JUDD: God Almighty!

MENZIES: If you play your cards right he may put you
in his weekly column. The public school
communist as a sign of the times. Must be worth
a paragraph at least. Shall we tidy up a bit?

JUDD: No! I'm working!

MENZIES: All work and no play —

JUDD: I *want* to be dull! Can't you understand?
Revolution is made by dull people doing dull
things with tremendous thoroughness and
discipline!

MENZIES: But once the revolution comes — they're
heroes of the people. Not to say commissars.
[JUDD *pretends to go on working.*] You couldn't be
dull if you tried. Boring, but not dull.

JUDD: Thanks a lot.

MENZIES: Don't you bore yourself sometimes, being the
prophet in the wilderness?

JUDD: It's only one more term.

MENZIES: I want to talk to you about that, actually. [*He moves* BENNETT's *books aside to perch on the table.*] Oh, God, jam on his notebook! Must be Bennett! It is!

JUDD: The answer is *No*.

MENZIES: I wish you'd reconsider.

JUDD: I wish you'd let me work.

MENZIES: Savanorola Judd, the scourge of the school! You must feel pretty isolated.

JUDD: I've never felt anything but lonely since the day I came here. The same faces, day after day, year after year — And none I ever want to see again.

MENZIES: You'll be even more isolated next term. [JUDD *shrugs.*] You're also going to make life jolly awkward for the rest of us.

JUDD: Hard cheese.

MENZIES: Look — I won't ask you to do anything you don't want to. You'll only have to go through the motions — prep duty — dorms — roll call. Nothing really.

JUDD: Menzies! Have you the makings of a politician in you?

MENZIES: I'm really speaking as one friend to another.

JUDD: You *have*! Well, well! What would Vaughan Cunningham say! Personal relations poisoned by political ambition!

MENZIES: Well, when you get power, however little it may be, you do find — you'd find it yourself — you can't always keep private and public things apart.

JUDD: In this country you can't. The British ruling class is totally corrupt. In a communist society, personal feelings are entirely irrelevant.

MENZIES: Not even you can actually believe that. [JUDD *shrugs.*] We are friends, aren't we?

JUDD: I really don't know. Are we? We've known each other for a quarter of our lives. I don't actually *dis*like you. You probably don't actually *dis*like me. But I don't know if Vaughan Cunningham would regard four years of enforced mutual toleration as friendship, quite.

MENZIES: Damn Vaughan Cunningham! I want you to be one of my prefects!

JUDD: *Your* prefects! How very proprietary!

[*Knock at the door.* WHARTON *is there with a tray of tea-things.*]

MENZIES: Oh — Wharton. Good.

JUDD: What do you want?

WHARTON: To lay, please.

JUDD: You can't.

MENZIES: Judd —

JUDD: I'm Hon. Sec. of Library. No-one's informed me officially about this tea.

MENZIES: Come on!

JUDD: I wasn't even *consulted*!

MENZIES: I couldn't find you to consult you. Anyway, it's Farcical's orders.

WHARTON: Please, Judd!

[*He is almost dropping the tray.*]

JUDD: Oh, for God's sake, do what you bloody well like! Just don't disturb me! I'm working!

[*He resumes his book.* WHARTON *rests the tray on the edge of the table and looks doubtfully at* MENZIES.]

MENZIES: Judd —

JUDD: No. [*He looks at* MENZIES, *then at* WHARTON. *He softens.*] Oh, all right, all right! Lay away!

[*He sweeps up his books and papers, keeping the bust of Lenin under his arm like a soft toy.*]

WHARTON: Thank you, Judd.

JUDD: [*suddenly gay*] I say, cucumber sandwiches! How posh!

[*He takes one.*]

WHARTON: Oh, Judd, please!

JUDD: They're meant to be eaten, aren't they?

WHARTON: They're all arranged!

JUDD: I'll eat another, then, to balance. There! No-one'll notice. [WHARTON *looks reproachful.*] I'm sorry, but being angry makes me hungry. [*to* MENZIES] So now the old lecher gets a chance to corrupt our bodies as well as our minds.

MENZIES: There's to be no corruption. That's why I'm here. Come on Wharton.

    [*He starts helping to lay the table.*]

JUDD: Oh, you won't be able to stop him. One glance at our fresh pink faces, and his palsied hands will scurry to our fresh pink —

MENZIES: Judd!

JUDD: — knees, Menzies. Knees. Watch out for your cartilages. Some of these old crabs can give a fearful nip.

WHARTON: [*with the tray unloaded*] Excuse me, Judd.

JUDD: Yes?

WHARTON: Shall I make the tea now, or wait?

JUDD: Make it now.

WHARTON: But it may get cold.

JUDD: Then wait.

WHARTON: But then it may not have time to brew.

JUDD: No one'll notice. We'll all be too busy being impressed.

    [*He gestures with his fingers, like a crab pinching.*]

WHARTON: You think I should wait, then, or not?

JUDD: I think you should do whatever's most likely to make you least anxious.

WHARTON: Oh, but —

MENZIES: Wait, Wharton.

WHARTON: Thank you, Menzies.

JUDD: And whatever you do, when you grow up, don't go in for catering.

WHARTON: Of course I won't. We've been in timber since 1773.

    [MENZIES *laughs as* WHARTON *exits.*]

JUDD: That poor child! Do you know, he talks in his sleep? Orders his dog about, all night long. Come here! Sit! Fetch! Stop it! Good dog! And all day long he *is* the wretched dog. So anxious to please he's practically wetting himself. Not to give *dis*pleasure, rather.

MENZIES: Well, I follow the Barclay line. The less anxiety the better.

JUDD: A system built on force and fear will always have to be maintained, in the last resort, by force and fear.

MENZIES: Then we must see the last resort is never reached, mustn't we?

JUDD: Oh, yes, you're a good mild moderate. Given a proper education with some real people, you might have turned out quite a useful member of society.

MENZIES: Thanks!

JUDD: It's too late now, though. You'll have to go.

MENZIES: By the time you've finished, will there be anyone left?

JUDD: The whole country will be left!

[*He gives the clenched fist salute as* DEVENISH *enters with* VAUGHAN CUNNINGHAM, *a tall, straggly, slightly stooping man of 45–50. He has a bright tie, but his suit is well-worn. He looks mildly surprised at* JUDD's *salute.*]

CUNNINGHAM: Dear me!

DEVENISH: Oh, pay no attention. That's Judd. Our tame communist.

CUNNINGHAM: [*Shaking* JUDD's *hand before* JUDD *has time to remove it*] Not *too* tame, I trust?

DEVENISH: And this is Menzies. He's a prefect. But we let him in here sometimes, as he's not too bad.

CUNNINGHAM: How do you do, Menzies?

MENZIES: How do you do, Sir?

CUNNINGHAM: So this is where you fellows sit, is it?

JUDD: It's where we work. Between interruptions.

DEVENISH: Judd —

CUNNINGHAM: Oh, but aren't all interruptions welcome? They are with me.

DEVENISH: Ignore him. He's always like that.

CUNNINGHAM: Are you? Brusque and uncompromising? How splendid!

MENZIES: He'd work sixteen hours a day if we let him. We have to stop him for his own good.

CUNNINGHAM: Oh, I don't like the sound of that. When people claim to be doing things for other people's good, it always means their own. Don't you think?

MENZIES: Well, I — well —

CUNNINGHAM: And if you really are working, we mustn't disturb you.

JUDD: It's all right. We don't get a bang-up brew like this every day.

CUNNINGHAM: And it's worth putting up with almost anything for a bang-up brew! How I remember! Are you working for a scholarship?

JUDD: When I'm allowed to.

CUNNINGHAM: Oxford or Cambridge?

JUDD: Cambridge.

CUNNINGHAM: Well, it always was the one for the puritans.

DEVENISH: Take that, Judd!

CUNNINGHAM: But it was. All those tiresome people who made life difficult for Queen Elizabeth. And nothing seems to have changed. I've a nephew at King's — which college are you going to?

JUDD: Trinity.

CUNNINGHAM: Well, he's rather too social for you, I think. And you're certainly too socialist for him. He says everything's drearily political these days. No fun at all.

JUDD: [*dry*] No.

CUNNINGHAM: When *I* was an Apostle, it was all G.E. Moore — 'the pleasures of human intercourse, and the enjoyment of beautiful objects.' Some of us said, why not combine the two and enjoy the pleasures of intercourse with beautiful human objects? But that was before the war, of course, when it was still all right to make jokes. Flippancy's very much frowned on now, one hears.

JUDD: One must certainly hope so, mustn't one?

MENZIES: Did you know G.E. Moore personally, Sir?

CUNNINGHAM: *Did* I! I *do!* He's still quite a young man. [*They look at him with incredulity.*] Well — one's ideas of youth and age become more flexible as one grows older, you know. But he's only in his fifties. The greatest single influence on my life. Greater than Jesus Christ. Greater even than the Kaiser.

[*Polite laughter. A knock at the door.*]

DEVENISH: Come in!

[WHARTON *appears, staggering with a huge teapot.*]

Oh, thanks, Wharton.

WHARTON: [*putting down the teapot*] Shall I bring the muffins now?

[*He addresses the question to* JUDD.]

JUDD: Don't ask me. It's not my party.

MENZIES: [*seeing* WHARTON's *anxious look towards him*] Yes, please.

[WHARTON *goes.*]

CUNNINGHAM: Did he say muffins? How wonderful! And look at all those sandwiches! You certainly do yourselves well. I hope no one missed my lecture to prepare them.

JUDD: Naturally.

CUNNINGHAM: How very kind!

JUDD: It wasn't kind. He was told to.

CUNNINGHAM: Well, how kind of someone to tell him, and how kind of him to obey. And who is this?

[BENNETT *has entered, carefully spruced up, with a clean shirt, etc.*]

BENNETT: I'm sorry I'm late, Sir. Bennett — Guy Bennett. I was arguing with some people about your lecture. I couldn't get away. [*To the others this is a transparent lie.*] I thought what you said — I thought it was absolutely illuminating.

CUNNINGHAM: Thank you! One likes to think one raises the blinds a little, lets in a chink — a little ray.

DEVENISH: Let's sit, shall we? Uncle Vaughan — you sit here.

JUDD: [*in passing, to* BENNETT] You little toady!

BENNETT: [*to* JUDD] Shut up — and *sit*.

[JUDD *sits ostentatiously away from the party, in the window-seat.*]

CUNNINGHAM: Thank you. [*sitting*] One remembers so well how dark and dreary adolescence is. Confusion of mind worse confounded by utter confusion of body. Even one's voice suddenly betrays one. And one's passions are so random and unreliable — cricket scores one minute, Swinburne the next. I don't suppose any of you read Swinburne?

BENNETT: I'm afraid not, Sir.

MENZIES: Not a set book!

CUNNINGHAM: Well, nor do I now. But when I was your age — [*putting on a tremendous poetry voice*]

Could you hurt me, sweet lips, though I hurt you?
    Men touch them and change in a trice
The lilies and languors of virtue
    For the raptures and roses of vice.

BENNETT: Wow!

CUNNINGHAM: Well, that's rather what we thought at the time. Of course we were sensationally innocent. The very word 'vice' was enough to make us blush. Now I suppose you say 'fuck' and 'bugger' the whole time.

[*Utter consternation among the boys, into which* WHARTON *enters with the muffins.*]

Oh, the muffins! Delicious! And who is the Ganymede?

DEVENISH: What?

MENZIES: His name's Wharton, Sir.

CUNNINGHAM: Well, *thank you*, Wharton. Thank you *very* much.

WHARTON: [*highly embarrassed*] Is there anything else?

MENZIES: No, thanks. Thanks, Wharton.

[WHARTON *goes hurriedly.*]

CUNNINGHAM: [*taking a muffin handed by* DEVENISH] Curious little man, Swinburne. A gnome. Wonderful red hair, but the head too big for the body. The sordid truth will come out eventually, I suppose.

BENNETT: What sordid truth is that, Sir?

CUNNINGHAM: He never got over being swished at Eton. Obsessed with it all his life. Harold Nicolson tries to make out it's all exaggerated, but it's not. Not at all. I've seen some of the letters, and I can tell you — hot stuff.

BENNETT: Why would Mr Nicolson want to conceal it, Sir?

CUNNINGHAM: Oh, ambition — wouldn't you think? One doesn't get on in the Foreign Office by publishing dirt about eminent men of letters. Mild scandal, yes. But not dirt.

MENZIES: Why does he write about Swinburne at all, if it's so awkward?

CUNNINGHAM: If you ask me, he's secretly intrigued. He started with Verlaine, you know — then Tennyson, then Byron. There's a lot of very thin ice there. Of course, Harold's very nippy on his skates. But I rather think we'll find him giving up literature now he's going into politics. You can get away with much more at the FO than you can in the House of Commons.

BENNETT: I'm going into the FO.

CUNNINGHAM: Are you? Well, it's an excellent way of seeing the world, if you can stand all the ghastly dinners with the other diplomats.

BENNETT: I hadn't thought of that!

DEVENISH: Have another ghastly muffin.

CUNNINGHAM: No thank you!

[*Awkward pause.*]

BENNETT: What did you mean about Tennyson, Sir?

CUNNINGHAM: Tennyson?

BENNETT: I thought he was terribly respectable.

CUNNINGHAM: Well — Arthur Hallam. In Memoriam. [*to* JUDD] They were both Apostles in the early days, you know.

BENNETT: Oh, dear! [*smiling*] Is no one's reputation safe?

CUNNINGHAM: [*smiling back*] Well, I've always said it was complete nonsense about Queen Victoria and John Brown. [*Polite laughter.*] Is there much swishing here these days?

JUDD: Ceaseless.

MENZIES: Practically none, Sir.

CUNNINGHAM: Oh, I must say, one doesn't recall it as nearly so stimulating as Swinburne says.

MENZIES: As a matter of fact, I'm thinking of doing away with it in this house altogether. I'm head of house next term, you see.

> [*This statement causes a sensation among the other boys.*]

CUNNINGHAM: Well done!

DEVENISH: What's this?

MENZIES: As an experiment.

BENNETT: Well!

JUDD: [*mocking*] Well, well!

MENZIES: We must talk about it. I shall have to have the cooperation of my prefects, of course.

BENNETT: You've got mine already!

DEVENISH: Look here, you can't just spring it on us out of the blue like this. It's not the time or place.

CUNNINGHAM: Donald! Don't tell me you support the beating of little boys' bums!

DEVENISH: I'm not sure. I don't see any point in change for change's sake.

CUNNINGHAM: But this would be for the sake of the bums!

MENZIES: I think there's rather more to it than that, Sir. It's not just the pain given — there's also the pleasure of the one doing the beating.

CUNNINGHAM: Really! I had no idea. [*He had every idea.*]

JUDD: Menzies, you've been opening books again! You mustn't do it. You'll start thinking, and then where will you be?

MENZIES: If all that stuff's true —

JUDD: Of course it is.

BENNETT: Haven't you ever seen Fowler's — [*He just stops himself in time.*]

CUNNINGHAM: [*all innocence*] Fowler's what?

BENNETT: Fowler's a prefect, Sir. He — he gets excited when he's beating someone.

CUNNINGHAM: Dear me!

BENNETT: Uncontrollably, sometimes.

DEVENISH: Bennett — do you mind?

MENZIES: Yes, I'm sure Mr Cunningham isn't interested in —

CUNNINGHAM: Oh, but I am! I'm riveted! I shall write an article!

DEVENISH: Don't you dare.

CUNNINGHAM: Oh, I won't mention the school by name. What further revelations have you for me?

BENNETT: [*grinning*] Where shall I start?

MENZIES: [*quickly*] Of course some schools have abolished it already.

DEVENISH: Only ludicrous places like Bedales and Dartington Hall. It's all rot. Beating's all right, so long as there aren't bullies.

JUDD: But there always are.

CUNNINGHAM: Do *you* get a thrill from it, Donald?

DEVENISH: Of course not. But you know where you are with beating. You do something — you get caught — that's three, four, six strokes, depending. And then it's over. It's short, and it's sharp.

JUDD: And it's savage.

CUNNINGHAM: I thought communists were all for discipline.

JUDD: Discipline, yes. Barbarism, no.

DEVENISH: Well, since you're not going to be a prefect, what you think makes no difference, luckily.

CUNNINGHAM: Oh, dear! Have you offended authority with your revolutionary views?

JUDD: I refuse to collaborate with a system of repression.

CUNNINGHAM: Splendid! I *am* impressed!

DEVENISH: You're meant to be.

JUDD: You're so corrupt, you can't believe anyone *could* actually do something on principle, can you?

CUNNINGHAM: *Are* you, Donald?

DEVENISH: I know showing off when I see it. Judd doesn't realise he's here to learn, not teach.

JUDD: You'll *never* learn. Not till they put you in front of a firing squad.

CUNNINGHAM: Oh, dear! Is there no hope for him at all?

JUDD: If people align themselves with the forces of progress — well and good. If they don't — History will take care of them.

CUNNINGHAM: History! Does the individual count for nothing, then?

JUDD: Very little. Though the *object* of the revolution is, of course, to increase the general level of human happiness.

CUNNINGHAM: Will it increase mine, do you think?

JUDD: If you let it. If you persist in your cult of bourgeois individualism, your middle-class selfishness and egotism, obviously not.

CUNNINGHAM: How very severe. So people like me are to be crushed beneath your chariot wheels, are they?

JUDD: We shall have tanks.

CUNNINGHAM: You know — I hate to say this — but you sound just like the people who sent me white feathers in the war.

MENZIES: Did they really, Sir?

DEVENISH: Oh, Lord, don't let's go into that.

BENNETT: Why not?

CUNNINGHAM: There was a certain amount of friction between my sister and his father. Feathers flew in all directions, and not only white ones. I was expelled from the bosom of the family. Not that it was anything but a lumpy, bumpy sort of place at the best of times. Donald's father was so ashamed of me, he wouldn't even let me labour on his land. I had to go and labour in Monmouthshire. That's *all* lumps and bumps.

DEVENISH: It's very nice, Monmouthshire.

BENNETT: I must say, Sir — it's hard to think of you as a horny-handed son of toil.

CUNNINGHAM: I'm glad the whiff of the bull-pen no longer trails about me. Sometimes I think it does. I have to go and have a bath. I'm sure there's some doleful Freudian explanation — something unmentionable to do with my potty, I expect. You all read Freud, I suppose?

BENNETT: Lord, no! We're not allowed stuff like that.

CUNNINGHAM: Not even under the blankets?

JUDD: Fat chance!

CUNNINGHAM: Well, perhaps it's as well. He's as depressing as Karl Marx.

JUDD: What's *that* supposed to mean?

CUNNINGHAM: More depressing, really. One can at least struggle against historical forces. One can lie down in front of the juggernaut, as it were, and try to slow its progress.

JUDD: You do recognise that it *is* progress, then!

CUNNINGHAM: [*not to be deflected*] But one can't lie down in front of one's subconscious. One can't even *find* it to lie down in front of. And if that really controls everything we do — Well, I call it a very gloomy view. One likes to think one has some control over one's life. For instance, I'd like another cup of tea, please, Donald.

DEVENISH: Oh — sorry.

CUNNINGHAM: Thank you, dear boy. I can't bear to think it's either History *or* my subconscious that's making me thirsty. Any more than I can bear to think I spent two subaqueous years uphill and down dale in Monmouthshire simply at the whim of my id or — the forces of progress, do you call them?

JUDD: Yes.

CUNNINGHAM: You see, *I* thought there was a moral principle involved. [*taking his tea*] Thank you. You know, I believe Judd would like a cup of tea.

[BENNETT *pours tea.*]

You see, I thought it was wrong to kill. An eccentric view in a Christian society, of course. But I believe one must obey one's moral intuitions, however eccentric, and however awkward the consequences. It's those intuitions that separate us from the animals — don't you think?

BENNETT: [*taking tea to* JUDD] Yes — of course.

CUNNINGHAM: You say, of course. But Judd doesn't think so. Nor does Freud. They say moral intuitions are all nonsense. So did the people who sent me feathers.

BENNETT: Did you get so very many?

CUNNINGHAM: I could have stuffed pillows. Well, not literally. But a good many, yes. From people so sure of the absolute rightness of their position, they felt no need to put their names to it.

BENNETT: That's pretty rotten.

JUDD: I'm quite prepared to put my name to my position.

CUNNINGHAM: Oh, I'm sure.

JUDD: So what's the connection?

CUNNINGHAM: You none of you allow any room for doubt. For me, doubt is the basis of all moral life. If you take away doubt and claim absolute authority, whatever name you give it, you diminish the humanity of man. You diminish mankind.

[*Pause.*]

MENZIES: But you had no doubt you were right to be a conscientious objector.

CUNNINGHAM: I had ceaseless doubts. I was always open to argument. Indeed, I had to be. The local labourers took a very poor view of me. But there's no argument with History, is there?

JUDD: No.

CUNNINGHAM: And that doesn't worry you?

JUDD: Why should it? It's a fact.

CUNNINGHAM: Oh, dear!

DEVENISH: You'd have looked pretty silly if the Germans had invaded.

CUNNINGHAM: Oh, Donald! You're such a chip off the old block! [*to the others*] He'll make a splendid lord of the manor, won't he? Riding round in a tweed cap, just like his father, frowning at the farmers. [*to* DEVENISH] They'll adore you, absolutely adore you.

DEVENISH: They'd better!

CUNNINGHAM: The Devenishes have been there since 1543, you know.

DEVENISH: 1547, actually. More tea?

CUNNINGHAM: No, thank you. I've done *very* well.

BENNETT: [*who has been waiting his chance*] Sir —

CUNNINGHAM: Dear boy?

BENNETT: There was something in your lecture — you said, nothing in the world was certain except our feelings. The — intuitions and so on.

CUNNINGHAM: Yes?

BENNETT: But feelings change. Mine do, all the time.

CUNNINGHAM: Yes, indeed.

BENNETT: Then — well — how do you hold on to anything?

CUNNINGHAM: Why should you want to?

BENNETT: But — you must have something.

CUNNINGHAM: Why?

BENNETT: Well — it's chaos otherwise.

CUNNINGHAM: Yes. But — [*in his quotation voice again*] 'Every moment some form grows perfect in hand or face; some tone on the hills or the sea is choicer than the rest; some mood of passion or insight or intellectual excitement is irresistibly real and attractive to us — for that moment only.' You know your Pater, I hope?

BENNETT: [*confused*] He's dead.

CUNNINGHAM: *Walter* Pater — *The Renaissance.* 'Not the fruit of experience, but experience itself, is the end.' Oh, you must read it, you really must. He says the purpose of life is to be always at the place where the greatest number of vital forces unite in their purest energy. 'To burn always with this hard gem-like flame, to maintain this ecstasy, is success in life.'

[*Pause.*]

BENNETT: That's wonderful.

JUDD: [*rising*] Is it all right if I go and be sick now?

MENZIES: Judd —

[*But* JUDD *walks out.*]

I'm awfully sorry, Sir. He —

CUNNINGHAM: Oh, but it's the greatest compliment I've been paid in years! To annoy someone so much he leaves the room!

BENNETT: I must read Pater. 'To burn ever —'

CUNNINGHAM: Always. 'To burn always with this hard gem-like flame —' Of course Judd thinks History will snuff out our little flames like that! [*He snaps his fingers.*] But I think I'd rather be snuffed out while ecstatic, than gutter down quietly in slavish obedience to its dictates.

DEVENISH: All that's very fine and large, but —

[*The house bell rings.*]

CUNNINGHAM: Oh, dear, what does that mean?

MENZIES: [*rising*] Only that I have to go and take roll-call, if you'll excuse me, Sir. I'll answer for you two.

DEVENISH: Thanks.

BENNETT: Thanks.

MENZIES: It's been fascinating listening to you, Sir. Really fascinating.

CUNNINGHAM: Oh, the pleasure's been mine. It's not often I have the chance to show off to such a charming and attentive audience.

> [*Not sure what to make of this*, MENZIES *goes.*]
> Donald, is it time I went?

DEVENISH: The taxi'll be here in five minutes, Uncle Vaughan.

CUNNINGHAM: My hat? Where did I put my hat?

DEVENISH: You must have left it with the House Man.

CUNNINGHAM: Mr Farcical? Is that what you call him?

BENNETT: Among other things.

CUNNINGHAM: Donald, he did bristle at me so. I don't think I can face him again.

BENNETT: He bristles because he wasn't in the war and thinks he should have been.

CUNNINGHAM: I certainly got the impression he thought *I* should have been. Donald, be a dear, and rescue it.

DEVENISH: All right! Shan't be a minute.

> [DEVENISH *goes.*]

CUNNINGHAM: Such a — such a very — Is Donald quite as bluff and straightforward as he seems?

BENNETT: Oh, yes, Sir. He's got a perfectly good brain, actually, but he doesn't think it's gentlemanly to use it.

CUNNINGHAM: Oh. [*Pause.*] Bachelors always have such high hopes of their nephews and nieces. You're not afraid to use your brain, anyway!

BENNETT: No, Sir. [*Pause.*] It's a pity you're not staying longer.

CUNNINGHAM: Oh? [*Pause.*] Oh!

BENNETT: We could have had dinner. Gone on talking.

CUNNINGHAM: I could have gone on showing off, you mean! Though you young people have a good deal more to show than me!

BENNETT: I don't mind exhibiting myself.

CUNNINGHAM: Really? Well — perhaps we could continue our conversation some other time.

BENNETT: I should love that, Sir. And we do have holidays.

CUNNINGHAM: So you do. Where do you live?

BENNETT: Epping. Just on the edge of the forest.

CUNNINGHAM: I don't know Epping. [*giving him a card*] But if you ever come up to town —

BENNETT: Thank you, Sir.

CUNNINGHAM: Telephone first, won't you? One never knows when one's going to be free.

BENNETT: Of course, Sir.

CUNNINGHAM: My dear boy — no need to call me Sir. [*smiling*] I've one or two friends might amuse you. Harold, for instance.

BENNETT: Harold?

CUNNINGHAM: Nicolson.

BENNETT: Oh, that would be — May I bring a friend?

CUNNINGHAM: One of these?

BENNETT: No. Someone else. Someone — special.

CUNNINGHAM: By all means! [*Pause.*] Judd wouldn't like to come, would he?

BENNETT: I'm afraid not.

CUNNINGHAM: Pity. That sort of frankness is so attractive. So manly.

BENNETT: I'm afraid his interests lie elsewhere.

[DEVENISH *enters with* CUNNINGHAM's *hat.*]

DEVENISH: Whose lie where?

BENNETT: [*smooth*] Judd's. I was telling Mr Cunningham how Judd thinks literature is bosh, and we all ought to do economics.

DEVENISH: Oh, Judd! Come on, Uncle Vaughan. The taxi's early. There's time for you to buy me a drink on the way to the station.

CUNNINGHAM: Oh, dear! There's only one thing you young men can think of! Goodbye, Bennett.

BENNETT: [*shaking hands briskly*] Goodbye, Sir.

CUNNINGHAM: Come on, then, Donald!

[DEVENISH *and* CUNNINHAM *go.* BENNETT *does a little jig of delight.* WHARTON *enters with a tray, catching him at it.*]

BENNETT: What do you want?

WHARTON: I've come to clear.

BENNETT: Carry on, then!

[*He begins putting sandwiches in his pockets.*]

WHARTON: Hey!

BENNETT: What?

WHARTON: Those are fags' perks!

BENNETT: Fags don't have perks after *Library* tea, Wharton.

WHARTON: Bennett!

BENNETT: [*pushing the plate of sandwiches over*] Here — have these and think yourself lucky.

WHARTON: But there's the char-wallah! And the slicers and butterers!

BENNETT: Tell them Mr Cunningham ate everything up.
[*He goes to get the binoculars.*]

WHARTON: That's not fair!

BENNETT: Too bad.

WHARTON: I'll tell Menzies!

BENNETT: Wharton, if you're going to clear — clear.
[*He goes to the window and raises the glasses.*
WHARTON *angrily bangs cups and saucers on to the tray.*]
If you carry on banging plates like that, I'll bang your — [*He stops, then whispers:*] Oh, my God!

WHARTON: [*alarmed*] What?

BENNETT: It's him!

WHARTON: Who?
[*Pause.*]

BENNETT: [*lowering the glasses*] Oh, God, I can't look.
[*He slumps to the window-seat.*]

WHARTON: Are you all right, Bennett?

BENNETT: I will be in a moment.

WHARTON: Shall I get Matron?

BENNETT: It was his smile. It made me dizzy. It's slightly off-centre, you know. [*He turns and raises the glasses again.*] Everything beautiful is slightly lop-sided.
[MENZIES *enters but* BENNETT *doesn't see him.*]
There's a little hollow at the base of his throat

which makes me want to pour honey all over him, and lick it off again.

MENZIES: [*furious*] Bennett!

BENNETT: [*not looking round*] Hello.

MENZIES: Wharton — why isn't this table cleared?

WHARTON: Menzies, Bennett's taken fags' perks!

MENZIES: Is that any reason not to clear the table?

WHARTON: It's not fair! They're ours! It's house practice.

MENZIES: Bennett, what have you done with Wharton's perks?

BENNETT: [*still looking out*] Earth hath not anything to show more fair. Nothing at all.

MENZIES: [*crossing and snatching the binoculars away*] Stop that!

BENNETT: Give those here!

MENZIES: What have you got in your pockets?

BENNETT: Oh, for God's sake! [*He pulls out the sandwiches and throws them onto the table.*] Here! Now give me those back.

MENZIES: Certainly not.

WHARTON: [*examining the sandwiches*] They're all squashed!

BENNETT: Menzies, will you please give me those binos.

MENZIES: I'm confiscating them.

BENNETT: What the hell are you talking about?

WHARTON: They've got *fluff* on them!

MENZIES: Wharton, if this table is not cleared in one minute, you'll be up before Barclay for six strokes.

WHARTON: [*clearing rapidly*] Yes, Menzies.

BENNETT: I thought you were supposed to be against corporal punishment.

MENZIES: Hurry up, Wharton.

> [BENNETT *turns his back on* MENZIES *and goes back to the window, staring out.* WHARTON *hastily gathers plates and cups to the tray.* MENZIES *goes and holds the door open for him.*]

WHARTON: [*going*] Thank you, Menzies.

MENZIES: [*shutting the door*] Have you completely lost your mind?

BENNETT: Yes, actually.

MENZIES: After all that's happened, you talk like that in front of a junior!

BENNETT: He doesn't understand.

MENZIES: Of course he does!

BENNETT: You don't understand, either. I'm in *love*, Jim.

MENZIES: Don't talk such utter piffle. And taking fags' perks! That's a filthy trick. [BENNETT *laughs*.] It's not funny. You'd better take a pull on yourself.

BENNETT: I'd rather do it with you.

MENZIES: For God's sake, will you stop it! [*He is very angry*.] I'm warning you, Guy, you carry on like this, and I'll be looking for someone else to be my number two.

BENNETT: Sanderson? Don't be ludicrous.

MENZIES: You don't know what's going on. Devenish may be leaving.

BENNETT: What?

MENZIES: *Fowler* may be going to stay on. [BENNETT *is stunned*.] I thought that might bring you to your senses. Now perhaps you'll stop this stupid nonsense and start behaving like a responsible citizen.

BENNETT: It can't be true.

MENZIES: It can be. It is. [*Pause*.] I'm not going to stand for it, of course. But I shan't be able to resist unless I have full cooperation from you and Judd.

BENNETT: *Judd*?

MENZIES: Why do you think I said that about beating? I *have* to have another prefect.

BENNETT: My God! You are getting sly!

MENZIES: You need him, too. If Fowler's head of house, *you* won't be in Twenty Two.

[*Pause*.]

BENNETT: God.

MENZIES: You're more Judd's friend than I am. I've tried and tried. It's useless.
[*Pause.*]

BENNETT: I shouldn't think there's a hope in hell.

MENZIES: There must be. Prove your worth for once.

BENNETT: Why's Devenish leaving?

MENZIES: Martineau.

BENNETT: Oh, Christ.

MENZIES: I hope I can rely on you. The next few weeks are going to be absolutely crucial. We can't afford the slightest *hint* of scandal. You really are going to have to take a — take —

BENNETT: Myself in hand? [*Pause, moving about*] The trouble is I do so much prefer doing it with other people. Don't you?

MENZIES: I don't believe in talking about it.

BENNETT: It's not the impression I've got when we've done it together.

MENZIES: I said, I don't believe in talking about it. [*Pause.*] Besides, I think we're a bit old for that sort of thing now. We're supposed to be grown up.

BENNETT: Supposed by whom?

MENZIES: It's only a passing phase. All the books say so.

BENNETT: You *have* been reading! Worried, were you?

MENZIES: Weren't we all? [BENNETT *just looks at him.*] As a matter of fact I met a girl last hols.

BENNETT: Congratulations. Did she let you do anything?

MENZIES: I think she would have done. There wasn't the opportunity.

BENNETT: Ah!

MENZIES: We — fondled. [*Pause.*] The trouble is, girls of our age aren't very interested in us. We don't have any money.

BENNETT: Or cars.

MENZIES: I'm learning to drive. That should help. Take her to the flicks!

BENNETT: Will her parents let you?

MENZIES: Hope so.

BENNETT: Bet they won't. Parents don't give a damn about

their sons. They can be done all ends up with barge-poles. But their daughters! Offer to help a girl across the road and that's ten years' penal servitude for rape.

MENZIES: Well, but you can understand why. Girls can't look after themselves.

BENNETT: You think we can?

MENZIES: Of course.

[*Pause.*]

BENNETT: Martineau couldn't.

MENZIES: Well — [*Pause.*] I do make myself clear?

BENNETT: Oh, yes. Even if we're not actually grown up — whatever that may mean — we must act like it.

MENZIES: Precisely.

BENNETT: All right, then. Let it be charades! I say! What a ghastly turn up for the book.

MENZIES: Yes.

[*Pause.*]

BENNETT: May I have the binos back now, please?

MENZIES: [*handing them back*] Just do try to be sensible.

BENNETT: Thanks. [*looking out*] I think perhaps I'll be a spy when I 'grow up'.

MENZIES: You couldn't keep a secret for two minutes.

BENNETT: You'd be surprised. [*Pause.*] You can't beat a good public school for learning to conceal your true feelings. [*He lowers the glasses.*] What was for house tea today?

MENZIES: Toad in the hole.

BENNETT: Hell! And I missed it!

MENZIES: You don't like toad in the hole. Last time you said it was like fried toe-jam in flannel.

BENNETT: That's what I *said*, yes. What I really thought — I'd make a very good spy, actually.

[*The door opens abruptly. It's* FOWLER.]

FOWLER: There you are!

MENZIES: Yes?

FOWLER: Bennett!

BENNETT: [*pretending to look round*] Where?

FOWLER: Have you done your brasses yet?

BENNETT: I don't wear brasses. I'm not a horse.

FOWLER: Where's your belt? I want to see it. All your webbing. And your cap badge.

BENNETT: Accoutrements of war are not permitted in Library, I'm afraid.

FOWLER: Well? Where are they?

BENNETT: Why?

FOWLER: Don't be silly!

MENZIES: Oh, God! Jacker Pot!

BENNETT: Jacker Pot? What's Jacker Pot?

FOWLER: I'm warning you, Bennett.

BENNETT: You're always warning me. You're a sort of Eddystone Light, Fowler. I don't know where you get the energy to keep flashing and flashing.

FOWLER: Where's your equipment? Come on.

BENNETT: In my cubicle.

FOWLER: Come on, then. I'm not having you let down the whole house.

BENNETT: It won't be the whole house, Fowler. Juniors aren't in the corps. Nor's Judd.

FOWLER: Don't mention Judd to me!

BENNETT: [*going with* FOWLER] Judd? Did you say Judd? Hang on a moment, I thought I heard you say Judd.

MENZIES: Don't forget to have a word with him!

[MENZIES *also leaves.*]

[*Lights down.*]

In the darkness we hear BARCLAY *reading the roll-call of the house, and the boys answering 'Sum'.*

Lights up again: moonlight.

SCENE THREE: Library

BENNETT *is standing by the window with his dressing-gown over his day clothes (though we don't yet know that).* JUDD *is sitting at the table in his pyjamas, thinking hard. Long pause.*

BENNETT: The moon shines bright: in such a night as this,
When the sweet wind did gently kiss the trees
And they did make no noise, in such a night,
Bennett, methinks, mounted the Gascoigne walls,
And sigh'd his soul toward the Longford tents,
Where Harcourt lay that night.
    [*Pause.*]
If you don't say something soon, I shall scream.
JUDD: I'm thinking.
    [*Pause.* BENNETT *raises the glasses again.*]
I do have my reputation, you know.
BENNETT: Your *what*?
JUDD: Ssh. I'm a school joke, I quite realise that. But I am, don't you think, a *respected* joke? Because I do at least stick to my principles. If I abandon them now —
BENNETT: You don't care what people think.
JUDD: About me personally, no. But they'll say — that's what we said all along. It *was* all just a form of showing off.
BENNETT: On the contrary. They'll see the means justifying the end. A triumph for Realpolitik.
JUDD: They'll say it was all a fake. They'll think *all* communists are fakes.
BENNETT: So what? They're the people you say have got to go anyway.
JUDD: There are always recruits to be made, even here.
BENNETT: I think they'll be profoundly grateful. Sacrificing your integrity for a higher cause — they'll think you positively noble.
JUDD: It's not what they say about Stalin.
BENNETT: Oh, well — Stalin!
JUDD: That man is sweating blood, night and day, to

drag his country into the twentieth century!
And to create a whole new *concept* of society at
the same time!

BENNETT: Ssh!

JUDD: I can't stand it when people sneer at him. Jokes
about the Czar in commissar's clothing. They
don't even *try* to understand the problems. You
can't judge Russia as though it was a so-called
liberal democracy with centuries —

BENNETT: Cave!

> [*They both dive for cover. Soft footsteps
> approach. The door opens. It is* BARCLAY,
> *fully dressed. He has a torch. He shines it
> round and finds* JUDD.]

BARCLAY: I thought I'd find you here. It's all right. I
couldn't sleep, either. [JUDD *slowly rises*.] Wharton's talking in his sleep again. That bloody dog
of his gets on my nerves. I thought I'd go
walkies myself. Want to come?

JUDD: Well — I'm not exactly dressed for walking,
actually. I was working.

BARCLAY: Oh, well, I won't disturb you. Would you like
my torch? It is yours.

JUDD: Thanks.

BARCLAY: This drainpipe's still all right, isn't it?

JUDD: I'm afraid I can't tell you.

BARCLAY: [*leaning out of the window, kneeling on the seat*]
Seems to be.

JUDD: Barclay — is Farcical really going to ask Fowler
to stay on?

BARCLAY: Things do get about, don't they!

JUDD: Is he?

BARCLAY: I don't know. I'm sorry to tell you, I don't
actually care. I've had enough. If it wouldn't
mean letting everyone down even worse than
I've done already, I'd leave tomorrow. House,
school, everything. None of it means anything
to me any more.

JUDD: You are in a bad way!

BARCLAY: I haven't slept for eight nights. I don't know whether I'm coming or going. Quite frankly, I've got to the pitch where I simply don't know why we bother.

JUDD: Who?

BARCLAY: All of us. Why we keep the whole thing going. None of us really believes in it.

JUDD: Oh. Because you're afraid to think of anything better.

BARCLAY: Is that it?

JUDD: You're afraid for your status, your money, your property. You're afraid to imagine a world without possessions.

BARCLAY: Perhaps we are. Yes. Very probably. Well — Leave the window open for me, won't you?

> [*He goes out through the window. After a moment* BENNETT *emerges from his hiding place.*]

BENNETT: My God, that man's really cracking up.

JUDD: Liberals always do under pressure.

BENNETT: Poor old Barclay!

JUDD: I've no time for him. He just wants a nice easy life, with a nice easy conscience, and he has no right to either.

BENNETT: Oh, but he's pretty decent.

JUDD: Not really.

BENNETT: You're a hard man, Tommy.

JUDD: I try to be. It's no use being *nice*. You must understand that, or you'll never get anywhere.

BENNETT: Oh, but all my life I've been wanting people to think of me as a really nice Guy!

> [*Pause.*]

JUDD: I'm going to bed.

BENNETT: Are you going to join the fight against Fowler?

JUDD: I don't know. I hate him so much — it's difficult to think clearly.

BENNETT: You're on the right lines, anyway.

JUDD: Judgements must be *objective*, Guy.

BENNETT: The objective fact in this case is, Fowler is absolutely objectionable. [JUDD *is silent.*] Please, Tommy.

JUDD: If you appeal to me as your friend, I'll never forgive you. Menzies tried that.

BENNETT: Oh.

JUDD: I don't mind it from him. He isn't a friend.

[*Pause.*]

BENNETT: Thanks.

JUDD: I need time.

BENNETT: There isn't much.

JUDD: Oh, God, and I shall be in a rage all day tomorrow, too!

BENNETT: Why? Oh — Jacker Pot!

JUDD: Militarism from twelve to half-past four! Little Haigs and Frenches strutting about! Farcical in his pathetic uniform! God!

[*Pause.*]

BENNETT: If I lose us Jacker Pot — will you agree to be a prefect?

JUDD: If you lose us Jacker Pot, you'll probably not be a prefect yourself. [*Pause.*] I'm going to bed. Good night.

BENNETT: I could do it, you know.

JUDD: I don't approve of quixotic gestures — however generous. *Realism*, Guy. *Realism.*

BENNETT: Good night.

[JUDD *goes.* BENNETT *waits a moment, then removes his dressing-gown. He has his day-clothes on underneath, and tennis shoes. He opens the window and slips out.*]

[*Pause. Blackout.*]

In the darkness there is a cacophony of cornet calls and military orders: 'Squad — shun! Right turn! About turn! Present arms!' etc, etc. The impression is of several squads being drilled by many different people. End with a final cornet call — 'Stand Easy'.

SCENE FOUR: Barclay's study

In the darkness, BARCLAY's *voice is heard over the final cornet call.*

BARCLAY: Fag!

> [*Stampede of feet. Then lights up on the study.* WHARTON *is at the door. All the prefects are present —* BARCLAY, DELAHAY, FOWLER, MENZIES, SANDERSON, *All are in Corps uniform, and of various ranks.* DELAHAY *sprawls on the window-seat, a sergeant.*]

Ask Bennett to come here. At once.

WHARTON: Yes, Barclay.

> [WHARTON *goes.*]

FOWLER: [*boiling with rage*] Thank you!

BARCLAY: I do wish you'd sit down.

FOWLER: Thank you! I prefer not!

BARCLAY: Well, stand easy, for God's sake.

> [FOWLER *remains rigid.*]

DELAHAY: [*groaning*] I never want to stand again! I've had a nail in my boot all day!

FOWLER: *You* were almost as bad as Bennett!

DELAHAY: What's that supposed to mean?

FOWLER: Slopping about when you were supposed to be marching!

SANDERSON: Fowler, it's all *over*.

FOWLER: I asked for bags of swank, and what did I get? A platoon sergeant like a pregnant penguin!

DELAHAY: If I wasn't so shagged, I'd punch you in the face.

BARCLAY: Please — this isn't a barrack room.

FOWLER: It's your fault!

BARCLAY: [*weary*] I'm sure.

FOWLER: But you don't seem to *care*! We've lost a pot we've held for the last three years, and you just don't *care*!

BARCLAY: No.

FOWLER: You're a disgrace to the school!

[BARCLAY *shrugs. Pause.*]

MENZIES: It's Farcical I'm sorry for. He puts so much store by Jacker Pot. Not having been in the army himself.

[*A knock at the door.*]

BARCLAY: Come in.

[BENNETT *enters. His uniform is very creased.*]

BENNETT: Did you want me?

BARCLAY: Fowler's asked permission to beat you.

BENNETT: General attitude or something special this time?

FOWLER: Filthy webbing, Brasso on your cap badge, creases in your trousers!

BENNETT: I thought we were supposed to have creases in our trousers.

FOWLER: Not like *that!*

BENNETT: [*looking at his trousers*] I'm sorry. When I put them under the mattress last night, I must have got them the wrong way round.

FOWLER: I warned you! I told you to do everything again!

BENNETT: I *did* do everything again.

FOWLER: You made it worse, then!

BENNETT: I'm afraid so.

FOWLER: *What?*

BENNETT: I'm afraid I made it all worse. Like you said.

[*Pause.*]

SANDERSON: He did it deliberately!

DELAHAY: Bennett — you didn't!

BENNETT: I'm hopeless with Brasso. I can only ever get a really good shine on my nails. Look.

[*He shows his nails.*]

DELAHAY: Let me see your belt.

BENNETT: You want me to undress in front of all these people?

DELAHAY: Give it here.

BENNETT: [*to* BARCLAY] Must I? [BARCLAY *shrugs.*] Well — all right!

[*He unbuckles his belt and hands it to*
DELAHAY. DELAHAY *looks at it then hands it to*
BARCLAY.]

DELAHAY: I reckon that's worth a full six strokes.

FOWLER: *Thank you!*

BARCLAY: [*with a sigh*] Why did you do it, Bennett?

BENNETT: Do what?

BARCLAY: You lost us the pot.

BENNETT: Oh, surely not just me. Not all on my own.

FOWLER: You were far and away the worst dressed
soldier on parade!

BENNETT: I'm not a soldier. I'm a schoolboy. So are you.

FOWLER: Come on, Barclay. Let's get it over with.

BARCLAY: Sanderson?

SANDERSON: Six.

BARCLAY: Menzies?

MENZIES: I think he *was* extraordinarily scruffy, even by
his own low standards.

BENNETT: And I thought you were my friend!

MENZIES: But unless we can prove it was deliberate —
Well, it'll look as though we're picking on one
person for what was, let's face it, a pretty dread-
ful performance all round.

FOWLER: But it was deliberate! He just admitted it!

BENNETT: I most certainly did not.

FOWLER: You lost us a hundred points at least!

BENNETT: Well, Delahay must have lost us just as many,
forming fours. You don't ask to beat him.

FOWLER: Barclay, are you going to allow —

BENNETT: Anyway, it's jolly unfair, using a civil authority
to punish someone for military offences. If I
deserve discipline, which in any case I dispute,
the Corps should do it, not the house. I should
have a court-martial.

SANDERSON: Don't talk such drivel! Court-martial! Honestly!

FOWLER: It was the house you let down!

BENNETT: I'm sure when we're in uniform we're not
members of the house, Barclay. We're part of the

second battalion of the school Corps. I think you
should take it up with the C.O.

FOWLER: Barclay, for God's sake —

MENZIES: He may have a point, you know.

FOWLER: People have often been beaten in this house for
dirty boots!

BENNETT: Not recently, thank God.

BARCLAY: [*helpless*] Delahay —

DELAHAY: I think it's all piffle. I don't care whether it's
with a civilian cane or a military swagger-stick
— he ought to get six. Look at his belt!

MENZIES: May I?

> [BARCLAY *hands the belt to him.* MENZIES *looks
> at it, then at* BENNETT. *Pause.*]

BENNETT: I deny it absolutely.

BARCLAY: All right. You can go ahead, Fowler.

FOWLER: About time!

BARCLAY: Four strokes.

FOWLER: Four? Six!

BARCLAY: [*tired*] Oh, all right — six, then.

FOWLER: Come on, Bennett! Into Hall!

BENNETT: I appeal to Twenty Two.

SANDERSON: [*sarcastic*] Of course!

BENNETT: It's my right.

DELAHAY: It won't do you any good.

BENNETT: It's still my right.

BARCLAY: All right. If you insist. Sorry, you three.

FOWLER: If you let him off —

DELAHAY: We won't.

> [FOWLER, MENZIES *and* SANDERSON *go.*]

BARCLAY: This is very silly, you know. It won't make any
difference.

BENNETT: I just thought you ought to know — if one
stroke of Fowler's cane lands on my arse, I shall
go straight to Farcical and tell him the names of
everyone I've done it with over the last three
years. That's all.

> [*Pause.*]

DELAHAY: You wouldn't dare!
BENNETT: Try me.
      [*Pause.*]
BARCLAY: You can't do this, Bennett.
BENNETT: I shall begin at the top. [*Pause.*] Can I go now?
BARCLAY: No, you certainly can *not*.
DELAHAY: Of all the filthy, dirty — blackmail!
BENNETT: Self-preservation, I'd call it.
DELAHAY: You bloody little — *tart*!
BENNETT: You never thought it bloody at the time.
DELAHAY: God, I'll thrash you myself!
BENNETT: It's only cheating, Delahay. No need to get so excited.
DELAHAY: I don't cheat!
BENNETT: You do deliberate fouls the whole time.
DELAHAY: I don't know what you're talking about!
BENNETT: Come on. We all know what goes on in the scrum, when you think the ref's not looking. And cricket. If there's a junior umpiring, you appeal loudly when you know the man's not out. You put shoe polish on the ball. My God, even when you're playing fives, you run into the other man deliberately.
DELAHAY: That's got nothing to do with it!
BENNETT: All you great games players cheat the whole time. Because you know perfectly well you can get away with it far more often than not.
DELAHAY: You're not getting away with this!
BENNETT: I think I am. It's only a game, Delahay. Aren't sportsmen supposed to be good losers?
      [BENNETT *goes.* BARCLAY *and* DELAHAY *look at each other.*]

      [*Blackout.*]

In the darkness, first birdsong, then the distant sound of a mower, then the sounds of cricket: bat on ball, a spatter of applause, 'Good shot', etc.

SCENE FIVE: Cricket field

Cricket noises continued as required. WHARTON *is sitting on the ground, eating an ice-cream and reading Wisden. He is in grey flannels and a white shirt and sweater.* SANDERSON *and* DELAHAY *enter, both dressed for cricket.*

SANDERSON: But why? I just don't understand.

DELAHAY: Well — he is in the sixth form.

SANDERSON: What's that got to do with anything?

DELAHAY: [*embarrassed*] Well —

SANDERSON: By the way, have you seen Fowler today? He's absolutely thrilled with you. I'm fairly ecstatic myself.

DELAHAY: Look — the thing is — he said he'd go to Farcical.

SANDERSON: So what? If Farcical had seen that belt, he'd have given him six himself.

DELAHAY: Not about that.

SANDERSON: About what then?

DELAHAY: Well — it seems Barclay and Bennett —

SANDERSON: *What?*

DELAHAY: Apparently.

SANDERSON: No! When?

DELAHAY: It doesn't matter *when*. They did, that's all.

SANDERSON: [*with a laugh*] No wonder Barclay wasn't keen on a clear-out.

DELAHAY: Well, you can see — there was nothing I could do.

SANDERSON: God, you have to admire Bennett, you really do. What a cad!

DELAHAY: He's the limit. The absolute utter limit.

SANDERSON: God, I'd love to have seen Farcical's face!

[*They stroll on, meeting* FOWLER *as they go.* FOWLER *is also dressed for cricket. He turns from them in disgust. They exit.* FOWLER *spots* WHARTON.]

FOWLER: Wharton!

WHARTON: Yes?

FOWLER: Aren't you supposed to be umpiring?

WHARTON: No.

FOWLER: Scoring, then?

WHARTON: Not till half-past.

FOWLER: Well — you've only got twelve minutes!

> [FOWLER *strides on, looking for trouble. He meets* JUDD *and* BENNETT *coming the other way, also in grey flannels and white shirts.* BENNETT *has the binoculars.* FOWLER *turns from them and goes off the other way.*]

JUDD: What I really *hate* about cricket is, it's such a damned good game.

BENNETT: Judd's paradox.

JUDD: Wharton! You're reading! Is this wise?

WHARTON: Only Wisden.

JUDD: The opium of the English middle classes!

BENNETT: [*mocking*] There's no doubt about it. Cricket is a fundamental part of the capitalist conspiracy.

JUDD: Obviously.

BENNETT: The proletariat is forced to labour in the field, while the bourgeoisie indulges in the pleasures of batting and bowling. The whole system derives from the lord of the medieval manor's wholly unjustified 'right' to the unpaid labour of villeins at haymaking and harvest.

JUDD: [*amused*] You know, you're really beginning to get the idea.

BENNETT: Thanks!

> [*He raises the glasses.*]

JUDD: Wharton, how many batsmen, beginning with P, opened for Somerset between 1890 and 1914?

> [*Short pause.*]

WHARTON: Seven.

JUDD: Right!

BENNETT: [*still looking*] How on earth do you know?

JUDD: I wasted my youth on Wisden. Now I find it a struggle to remember the names of all the members of the Supreme Soviet.

BENNETT: Senile already! [*still looking*] Ah! I thought so! On his way to school shop.
[*He waves with his free hand.*]

JUDD: You're drawing attention to yourself again. And he's not waving back.

BENNETT: Of course not.

JUDD: You should learn from his discretion.

BENNETT: Wait. You'll see. When he gets to the trees — [*Pause.*] There!

JUDD: Congratulations.

BENNETT: [*lowering the glasses*] Thanks. Love makes such a difference, you know. No feelings of guilt or shame. No sense of dirty little secrets. You feel — right, somehow.

JUDD: How nice.

BENNETT: Or in your case, left.

JUDD: [*clapping*] Good shot! By the way, I've decided that the greatest happiness of the greatest number will be best served if I *do* become a prefect.

BENNETT: [*overjoyed*] Tommy! [*He tries to embrace* JUDD.]

JUDD: Get off! On the terms set forth by Menzies, but with one extra condition. I won't take house prayers.

BENNETT: Oh, he won't care about that!

JUDD: My decision, I think you should know, has nothing whatever to do with your belt and trousers. [BENNETT *laughs.*] I think you were very silly. You should either refuse to have anything to do with the Corps, or play along with it. You've made yourself enemies.

BENNETT: Who cares?

JUDD: You won't get far in the Foreign Office if you can't be a bit more diplomatic.

BENNETT: The foul fiend Fowler felled at last! God!

Tommy, I love you! Let's go and tell Menzies!

JUDD: *I'll* tell Menzies. You stay here. I don't want you butting in while I'm conducting my negotiations.

BENNETT: He'll be thrilled! Thrilled as I am!

JUDD: Don't be so emotional. It's a purely logical decision.

[JUDD *walks off.* BENNETT *raises the glasses, then lowers them again.*]

BENNETT: Wharton.

WHARTON: Yes?

BENNETT: Would you like to earn yourself another ice-cream?

WHARTON: Wouldn't mind!

BENNETT: If you go to school shop, you'll find someone from Longford's there. Harcourt. Do you know him?

WHARTON: By sight.

BENNETT: [*giving him a note from his pocket*] Give him this. Here's a tanner. [WHARTON *hesitates.*] All right, then — a bob. [*He hands* WHARTON *the money.*]

WHARTON: Why are you so keen on Harcourt?

BENNETT: If you really don't know, I'm certainly not going to tell you.

WHARTON: I was looking at him in chapel this morning. It's worth being in the choir. You can watch almost everyone.

BENNETT: If you don't mind being gaped at yourself.

WHARTON: Oh, no-one looks at me.

[BENNETT *looks him up and down.*]

BENNETT: No.

WHARTON: I thought Harcourt looked absolutely dopey. He was yawning the whole way through the service.

BENNETT: Too many late nights, I expect.

WHARTON: What do you mean?

BENNETT: Never you mind. Hurry up, or you'll miss him.

[WHARTON *goes. There is a burst of clapping.*

BENNETT *looks at the cricket, then hurries off.*]

Hell, I'm in next!

[*After a moment,* MENZIES *and* DEVENISH *enter from the opposite direction.* DEVENISH *has white flannels and a blazer.* MENZIES *is dressed like the others — grey flannels and white shirt.*]

DEVENISH: I've told Spungin a thousand times not to follow balls outside the off stump.

MENZIES: What does that make it?

DEVENISH: Eighty-two for three.

MENZIES: Not too bad.

DEVENISH: No-one much to come, though. Bennett just slogs, and Barclay — well, look at the way he's walking in. He's lost his form completely.

MENZIES: Are you surprised?

DEVENISH: Yes, well — look, I'm awfully sorry about all this. But quite frankly, when my father asked me what it was I was staying on *for* — well, it was damned difficult to say.

MENZIES: You could be in First Eleven next year.

DEVENISH: It's a long time to wait, just on the off-chance. The Colts' wicket-keeper's just as good as I am, anyway. And you and Bennett will be running the house, not me.

[*Another burst of clapping.*]

There! What did I tell you? Barclay out first ball! You'd better go and get your pads on.

[*As they are going,* FOWLER *comes rushing on, waving* BENNETT's *note.*]

FOWLER: Menzies! Menzies, look at this!

MENZIES: What is it?

[*He takes the note and reads it.*]

FOWLER: Now I've got him! He can't get away this time!

MENZIES: Where did you get this?

FOWLER: He gave Wharton a shilling to give it to Harcourt! I knew something was up! Wharton was supposed to be scoring, and I caught him sneaking off to school shop! [*taking the note back*] I'm showing this to Barclay!

[FOWLER *rushes off again.*]

DEVENISH: [*mystified*] What on earth's all that about?

[*Pause.*]

MENZIES: Devenish — do you think it'd make any difference to your attitude — and to your father's attitude — if you told him you were going to be in Twenty Two next year?

[*Blackout.*]

In the darkness we hear the sound of boys being summoned by FOWLER *with the call 'Into Hall! Into Hall!' We hear the sound of feet going up a staircase. Then silence. Then the sound of someone being given six strokes with the cane.*

SCENE SIX: Library

It is evening. JUDD *is working. The door is flung open and* BENNETT *rushes in, throws himself on the window-seat and hides his face.* JUDD *gets quietly up and shuts the door, then goes back to the table. Pause.*

JUDD: Didn't the blackmail work this time?

BENNETT: [*muffled*] I couldn't use it.

JUDD: I don't see why not.

BENNETT: [*still hiding his face*] Because.

[*Pause.*]

JUDD: Because what?

BENNETT: [*turning his tear-stained face*] Because James has two more years here! And if I'd gone to Farcical they'd have reported him too!

JUDD: So what?

BENNETT: I couldn't do that! I *love* him!

JUDD: Guy —

BENNETT: [*sitting up*] You still don't believe me, do you?

JUDD: I think you may *think* you're in love with him.

BENNETT: Look — I'm not going to pretend any more. I'm sick of pretending. I'm — [*He can't find a suitable word.*] — I'm never going to love women.

JUDD: Don't be ridiculous.

[*Pause.*]

BENNETT: It's why Martineau killed himself. He'd known since he was ten, he told me. I didn't know. Well — I wasn't sure. Till James.

JUDD: You can't possibly know a thing like that at ten. Or now.

BENNETT: Oh, yes you can. [*Pause.*] It doesn't come as any great revelation. It's more like admitting to yourself — what you've always known. Owning up to yourself. It's a great relief. In some ways. [*Pause.*] All this acting it up — making a joke of it even to myself — it was only a way of trying to pretend it wasn't true. But it is.

JUDD: Of course it's not.

BENNETT: Tommy, when you come down to it, it's as simple as knowing whether or not you like spinach.

JUDD: I can never make up my mind about spinach.

BENNETT: Then perhaps you're ambidextrous.

JUDD: No, I am *not*!

BENNETT: You see? You know.

[*Pause.*]

JUDD: You can't trust intuitions like that.

BENNETT: What else is there? Are you a communist because you read Karl Marx? No. You read Karl Marx because you know you're a communist.

[*Pause.*]

JUDD: Well — I'm very sorry.

BENNETT: Thanks! If that's how friends react —

JUDD: What do you want me to do? Get a horsewhip?

BENNETT: [*standing and feeling himself*] Not after Delahay, thanks.

JUDD: Why Delahay?

BENNETT: Barclay's lost his nerve. And Delahay has a very whippy wrist.
[*Pause.*]

JUDD: I apologise. You're quite right. It was patronising and unforgivable.

BENNETT: But you couldn't help it, could you? In your heart of hearts, like Barclay and Delahay and Menzies and Sanderson — in spite of your talk about equality and fraternity — you really believe that some people are better than others because of the way they make love.

JUDD: There's complete sexual freedom in Russia.

BENNETT: That's not a lot of comfort at the moment, actually. [*Pause.*] Martineau killed himself because he simply couldn't face a lifetime of *that*.

JUDD: But you said it was a great relief, knowing.

BENNETT: Oh, don't you ever listen? I said, in some ways. It's also a life sentence. [*Pause.*] Poor Martineau! He was just the sort of pathetic dope who'd've got caught the whole time. Spent his life in prison, being sent down every few months by magistrates called Barclay and Delahay.
[*Pause.*]

JUDD: I'm sorry, but I don't see how you can be so sure about it.

BENNETT: Because I *love* him!

JUDD: Come on!

BENNETT: You've never been in love. You don't understand. [*Pause.*] Everything seems different. Everything seems possible. You can really believe life could be — it's so obvious! It's madness what we have now. Strikes and beating and Twenty Two and — how many unemployed are there?

JUDD: Three million, seven hundred and fifty thousand.

BENNETT: God, are there really?

JUDD: Yes.

BENNETT: Well — there must be a better way to run things. And when you're in love, it all seems so easy. [JUDD *looks disapproving.*] Don't cluck at me, Tommy. You don't know what I'm talking about. [*Pause.*] We've been meeting every night. In Gridley Field pavilion. We don't just — actually we don't more often than we do. We just — hold each other. And talk. Or not talk. Till dawn last night. [*Pause.*] Maintaining ecstasy.

JUDD: Is he getting beaten, too?

BENNETT: No, no. He never got the note. They couldn't pin anything on him. And after Martineau and Robbins — Barclay doesn't want anyone in Longford's even suspecting. [*Pause.*] I understand all about Martineau now. He was in love with Robbins, but Robbins wasn't with him.

JUDD: Don't let your imagination run away with you.

BENNETT: For Robbins it was just a game. Assignation — excitement — hands fumbling with buttons in the dark — all perfectly normal! School practice! But then poor Martineau — he went and told him. And Robbins was revolted — disgusted! He shoved him away. *That's* not what he'd come for! And Martineau knocked something over and Nickers came in to see what was happening and —

JUDD: Yes.

BENNETT: Robbins furiously buttoning. Martineau — sobbing and sobbing with his trousers down. [*Pause.*] Think of that for a lifetime. [*Pause.*] Think of the names. Pansy. Nancy. Fairy. Fruit. [*Pause.*] Brown nose.

　　　[*Pause.*]

JUDD: Do I detect just a touch of self-pity?

BENNETT: Probably.

JUDD: Fight it. Every time someone calls you a name — thump him.

BENNETT: Thanks! And spend my whole life locked up?

JUDD: The suffragettes didn't get the vote by whining.

BENNETT: Suffragettes!

JUDD: You have to change the fundamental social attitudes, Guy. You have to make people *see*. It always comes down to that.

BENNETT: It does with you.

> [*The door opens and* DEVENISH *comes in with* MENZIES. DEVENISH *looks slightly sheepish.* MENZIES *is cool.* BENNETT *goes and pointedly looks out of the window.*]

MENZIES: Oh, good, you're both here. I've got some news. It was very generous of you, Judd, to offer, but it won't be necessary now. You can keep your principles untarnished. Devenish is staying on after all.

DEVENISH: I never really wanted to leave. Cirencester won't be that much fun.

> [BENNETT *slowly turns and looks at* MENZIES, *realisation dawning.*]

MENZIES: I'm sure you're both delighted. No more Fowler! But — I've a disappointment for you, Bennett. Though it can hardly come as a surprise after recent events. Devenish is going to be my number two.

BENNETT: You *bastard*!

MENZIES: You really gave me no choice, Guy.

BENNETT: Don't you dare call me by my Christian name again. *Ever*.

MENZIES: I understand your feeling. I'm sorry — but there it is. I'm sure I can still count on your co-operation as an ordinary prefect.

> [BENNETT *turns away.*]

JUDD: [*to* DEVENISH] You were easily bought.

DEVENISH: Well — my father was in Twenty Two himself. When I told him — well —

JUDD: Oh, and your son will be in Twenty Two, I'm sure. And your son's son! Even unto the end of the school!

MENZIES: Look, we've saved the house from Fowler, we've saved your conscience —

JUDD: Oh, yes, all problems solved! For life! No commies, and no queers!

MENZIES: You really have no right to take that line, you know.

JUDD: You sanctimonious little —

MENZIES: Don't let's quarrel. We're all going to have to live together. Let's try and do it as amicably as possible. [*Silence.*] Well — I thought you should be the first to know. Perhaps we'll get a better reception from Farquharson, Donald.

JUDD: Oh, so it's Donald now, is it?

MENZIES: Come on.

> [DEVENISH *gives a half-apologetic shrug, then follows* MENZIES *out. Long pause.*]

BENNETT: Sorry. Now they'll say you really wanted to be a prefect all the time, but they managed to stop you.

JUDD: I took that risk into account.

BENNETT: Did you? Honestly?

JUDD: Of course. All actions can have various possible consequences. You have to look at things *objectively*, Guy.

BENNETT: [*bursting out*] Did you see how they looked at me? Did you *see*? Like a piece of snot!

JUDD: So much for personal relations as the basis of civilised life!

> [*Pause.*]

BENNETT: You know, when Delahay was beating me — I could see in his face, he was trying to flog me out of his memory. He won't succeed, though. I'll haunt the whole bloody lot of them!

JUDD: That won't do you much good.

BENNETT: Well, what will? *Objectively*? It's not much of a prospect, is it?

JUDD: It's not the end of the world.

BENNETT: Isn't it? When people like Menzies run the world, and you want to be ambassador in Paris?

[*in imitation*] 'Bennett? Oh, nice enough chap—
quite amusing actually. We had high hopes of
him once, but — oh, you heard. Not quite one
of us. Bogota, do you think? Perhaps not, no.
Isn't Haiti coming up? That's about his mark.
He was never in Twenty Two, you know. Only
ever a *house* prefect.' [*He ends savagely.*]

JUDD: There's no reason you have to be any kind of
prefect at all.

BENNETT: Yes, there is. If I'm spending the rest of my life
hiding my true nature from the rest of the
world, I'm taking every comfort that's going
while it *is* going.

JUDD: Oh, well, if that's your attitude —

BENNETT: Besides, being absolutely *objective*, it would dish
me once and for all, wouldn't it?

JUDD: You can't have things both ways, Guy.

BENNETT: What do you want me to do — march about the
streets shouting slogans with you? I wouldn't
get past the first pub. [*He picks up 'Das Kapital'*]
As for this — [*He drops it.*] Too heavy.

JUDD: Either you accept the system, or you try to
change it. There's no alternative.

BENNETT: [*suddenly gay*] Why not? Why not both? Pretend
to do one, while you really do the other? Fool
the swine! Play along with them! Let them think
what they like — let them despise you! But all
the time —

JUDD: Don't talk drivel.

BENNETT: [*dreamily*] I'd have the last laugh. I'd be re-
venged.

JUDD: That's just romantic twaddle. You wouldn't be
in the mess you are now if you had any discretion at all.

BENNETT: What better cover for a secret agent than
apparent total *in*discretion? [*He sits down, but
leaps at once to his feet again.*] Hell! [*He feels himself
with his hand.*] Blood. The *bastard*.

JUDD: Well, if you won't defend yourself in the logical manner —
[*He resumes his reading.*]

BENNETT: I'll get him. I'll get him somehow.
[JUDD *refuses to respond.* BENNETT *goes to the window and picks up the binoculars. He looks out, but can't concentrate. He glances over at* JUDD. *He comes back to the table and rests his hand on 'Das Kapital'*]
Wouldn't it be wonderful if all this was true?

JUDD: It is true.

BENNETT: Heaven on earth?

JUDD: No. Earth on earth. A *just* earth.

BENNETT: My trouble is, I prefer love to justice.

JUDD: That's pure Vaughan Cunningham. It sounds tremendous. It doesn't mean a thing.
[BENNETT *picks the book up. He goes slowly to the window, reading the first page. He sits, cautiously. He looks out towards Longford's. Then he looks at the book.*]

[*Very slow fade. As the lights go down, the Choir begins to sing.*]

And there's another country,
    I've heard of long ago,
Most dear to them that love her,
    most great to them that know;
We may not count her armies,
    we may not see her King;
Her fortress is a faithful heart,
    her pride is suffering;
And soul by soul and silently
    her shining bounds increase,
And her ways are ways of gentleness
    and all her paths are peace.

The End

Other plays by Julian Mitchell

AFTER AIDA   0 906399 68 8

After the triumphs of *Aida* and *The Requiem* in the early
1870s, the composer Verdi has retired to the country.
His two friends, Ricordi the publisher and Faccio the
conductor, convinced that Verdi should write another
opera, finally persuade him to collaborate with the
young librettist, Arrigo Boito, on a new work, *Otello*.
Originally starring Richard Griffiths.

"*[After Aida]* . . . has been conceived with wit and
clarity, written, designed and directed with singular
style, [and] is enacted with panache, infused with
quality!"

Sally Osman, Western Mail

FRANCIS   0 906399 53 X

"The setting is the thirteenth century, the subject is the
life of St Francis of Assisi, and one clear virtue of
Mitchell's treatment is that it serves as a salutory
correction to the traditional, if hazy, image of the gentle
Francis communing with birds and beasts. His struggles
to found and preserve an order based on poverty and a
literal reading of the Gospels in the face of the Church's
attempt to institutionalise and dilute his beliefs provide
a number of scenes where the collision of ideas gives a
much needed dynamic . . ."

Malcolm Hay, Time Out

". . . a grave and beautiful play . . ."

Harold Atkins, Daily Telegraph

For a free copy of our complete list
of plays and theatre books write to:
AMBER LANE PRESS
Church Street, Charlbury, Oxon OX7 3PR
Telephone 0608 810024